O RIVER OF GOD

A Tribute to
the Prophetic Life and Ministry of

Barbara Massie

Evangelist Barbara Massie

O RIVER OF GOD

A Tribute to
the Prophetic Life and Ministry of
Barbara Massie

Louise Flanders
Jay Hearn

O RIVER OF GOD

39 Alexander Street
Avoca, New York 14809

All Scripture quotations are from the
Authorized King James Version
of the Bible

Cover photo: Christopher Hannan

Printed in the United States of America
by Reed Hann Litho Co.
Williamsport, PA. 17701

Dedicated to the Memory of
Our Mother,
Margaret Elizabeth Massie
"Whose face ever reflected the radiance
of His Presence"

-Anne Massie

Acknowledgements

Without the help of our friends: Gail Atkins (and her late father, Preston Atkins), Julie Grove, and Marsha Worth, this tribute to Barbara Massie would have been impossible. Each one's contribution and editing skills were unique and invaluable. And most importantly, each of their lives were touched by Barbara's ministry.

Gail, who as a student at Pinecrest Bible Training Center, was privileged to have smelled the heavenly fragrance of His Presence which surrounded Barbara as she ministered, leaving a lasting fragrance of Christ upon her life.

Julie, who drank deeply from the river of living waters while a student at Pinecrest, today experiences the increasing flow of that great river of God's Spirit as she pastors her congregation in the Detroit, Michigan area.

Marsha and Tom Worth were Barbara's forever loyal and trusted friends. Their lives were a faithful support and strength to the sojourning prophetess; and their home at Pinecrest was always open to Barbara, as a haven or simply for fellowship and a cup of tea.

Our special thanks to Anne Massie, who was the inspiration behind this endeavor, organizing and supplying chronological data and family pictures. Her life-long love and dedication to her sister was the undergirding of Barbara's ministry.

CONTENTS

Part Three
Testimonies

PREFACE

The deep heart-desire of Anne Massie has been to put together a written tribute to the life of her late sister, Barbara Massie. Some of us who knew Barbara and experienced the blessing of God through her ministry have undertaken to help Anne see her desire fulfilled. We have gathered material from recorded messages in which Barbara tells how her own experiences in God and in ministry transformed her life and the lives of many others.

Barbara Massie, raised up by God as an evangelist and prophetess to the Body of Christ, carried a powerful anointing that released the Spirit of God like a river upon His people. Wherever she went, she introduced lives to the wonderful flowing river of God. Individuals, as well as whole congregations, were swept by the power of the Holy Spirit into the very presence of Jesus – there to be changed forever!

Barbara's passion was to have a ministry of changing lives, and God wonderfully answered the prayer of her heart! Those upon whom she laid her hands for prayer or who received the prophetic word through her lips testified that their lives were never the same again. Those who drank from the freely flowing river through her, found the Spirit of God meeting the dry and barren places of their lives. The wilderness areas of many hearts received the rain of the Holy Spirit and were transformed into fruitful fields.

In the words of Wade Taylor, founder of Pinecrest Bible Training Center in Salisbury Center, New York, "I know many, many who are serving the Lord today in ministry who relate their experience in God directly to Barbara Massie's influence upon their lives. The fact that they have a vision, a ministry, and a depth in God is attributed to her influence. Many testify that the direction of their lives was changed as they were apprehended by God through her ministry."

I met Barbara Massie while I was a student at Elim Bible Institute, Lima, NY. In the meetings she held there, the power of God and the spirit of worship would fill the chapel like a heavy cloud. During one of her services, I was caught up into His Presence in worship, for the first time losing consciousness of everyone around me. My spirit was released to worship Jesus in a freedom and abandonment I had never before known. Although I already had the baptism in the Holy Spirit, it was through her ministry I experienced a life-changing immersion into the ***Person*** of the Holy Spirit. Barbara introduced us to a new and higher dimension of the power and anointing of God, opening it up for us to enter into. At that time I found a new reality in God that has carried me from that day forth, and I will forever be grateful to the Lord for sending us His servant.

Barbara Massie was a yielded vessel unto the Lord and greatly used of Him. The Scripture says that God is no respecter of persons, and opportunities of effective ministry are available for anyone who will yield and abandon themselves in obedience to the hand of the Lord as it comes upon them. His desire is to use all of us for His glory.

It is our prayer that as you read the pages of this book, you will find the testimony of Barbara Massie's life to be not only a blessing in your own relationship with our Lord Jesus Christ, but also a spiritual challenge to reach out and embrace all He has for you in this hour.

Louise Flanders
Avoca, New York

Part One

Margaret & William W. Massie
(L to R) Anne, Willie, Margaret & Barbara

Life Of A Spiritual Trailblazer

by Anne Massie

Barbara Massie was the third of four children born to William and Margaret Massie in Glasgow, Scotland. I was born, the youngest in the family, two years after Barbara, joining her and our older sister Margaret and brother William. Not only were Barbara and I close in age, but we were life-long best friends. Through our years of traveling the globe together and living out of suitcases, we became a devoted team to each other and to the Lord. Wherever we went, we carried a message of hope, freedom and forgiveness in Jesus Christ.

Our mother, Margaret Elizabeth Gray, was born in Banffshire, Scotland. The sudden untimely deaths of her parents made her an orphan when barely the age of twelve. Mother's oldest sister then took the family of seven under her wing. Though none of her family were saved, a Christian Brethren woman helped our mother come to know the Lord; and at 16 she was converted and baptized in water in the Brethren church.

Our father, William Wilson Massie, was born in Aberdeen, Scotland. Joining the army at age 16, he fought in the South African War and later in the Boer War. After Father's discharge from the army, he became a member of the police force in Glasgow where he met Mother. Accompanying her to the Brethren meetings, he, too, came to know Christ, and soon became a respected leader of the youth in the church.

When Barbara was five years old, the Apostolic Church opened a full gospel ministry in the city of Glasgow. Our father went to the full gospel meetings with the intention of pointing out to the Apostolics their "error" in believing in the baptism in the Holy Spirit, which he — like all the members of the Brethren — declared was received at salvation. Instead of converting the Apostolics, he was also filled with the Spirit! Embracing this new move of God, our parents soon stepped out of the house of bondage and into revival. Our father, W. W. Massie, then became a pioneer in the full gospel movement, serving the Lord as pastor and overseer in various assemblies in the Glasgow area. As a child in school, Barbara remembered being teased about the "holy rollers" who went to those "spooky" meetings where they climbed the walls and walked across ceilings!

The hand of the Lord rested upon Barbara from early childhood, and at a tender age she was made aware of her calling to Him. She wrote concerning her personal experience of salvation:

> "I was brought up in a Christian home, a native of Glasgow. I was always conscious of my need of a Savior, but I could not understand what it meant to be saved from sin. (Psalm 103:10-15)
>
> "In Sunday school with others I made a public decision to serve Christ, but my heart and mind knew no rest or satisfaction. It seemed as if a dark cloud veiled my eyes and I could not penetrate or comprehend the truth of God's salvation.
>
> "At a special meeting in Glasgow, when I was twelve years of age, I gave myself to Christ. The darkness fled and the light of God's love poured into my soul. I remember the preacher was speaking on

> Legion and the demoniac whom Christ delivered. It so awakened me to the powers of evil at large that I was glad to surrender myself to the love and mercy of God at the end of the service.
>
> "Many times hardness and coldness of heart has come into my experience; but through striving and prayer, God has given me the power to stand. Having put my hand to the plow, there must be no turning back!"

Looking at our family's roots, we can see the Lord's preparation in Barbara's life. Our father, a leader in the Apostolic Church of Great Britain, was mightily used of God as an apostle to plant churches in the north of Scotland, thus opening many areas to Pentecost for the first time. With the help of his wife and family, he established many works, most of which are still flourishing. All of us children were musical, which was helpful in the revivals. Our mother who was an intercessor and prayer warrior, and a woman of great piety and holiness, had a profound spiritual influence upon our young family, especially Barbara's life.

In 1947 our parents were sent to Stafford, England by the Apostolic Church to pioneer a new work. Barbara and I stayed on another year in Glasgow to finish our nursing training, joining them later in Stafford.

Each year in August, our family attended the annual convention of the Apostolic Church in Penygroes, South Wales, where Barbara later attended Bible school. Barbara's life was touched and profoundly changed in 1951, when Apostolic pastors Fred Poole from the United

States and George Evans from Canada brought the "Latter Rain" blessing to England and Wales. Pastor Poole prophesied over Barbara that her preaching and prophetic voice would be heard around the world – and that prophecy was wonderfully fulfilled in her life.

As Barbara played the accordion and I the guitar, we were always asked to sing at the Penygroes conventions. In 1954, Pastor McLeod and his wife, our former pastors in Glasgow now pastoring in Canada, happened to be at the convention that year. Mrs. McLeod was a great singer, and Barbara said to her, "We've been asked to sing, but I haven't got a song!" "Oh," she said, "I have a chorus from Canada called, 'O River of God.' You can sing that and make up some verses to it."

During the convention, without any effort at all, the Holy Spirit gave Barbara the words and the music for the verses to "O River of God." When we were introduced to go up and sing, the anointing was terrific, especially at the point in the song where it says, "The deaf shall have hearing; the blind folk shall see." The pastors sitting on the platform behind us called out, "Girls, sing it again! Sing it again!" As we sang again, the people rose to their feet and the Holy Spirit fell, greatly blessing the convention.

After attending Bible school for one year, Barbara became one of the night sisters (nurses) for casualty and theatre (operations) at Stafford Infirmary, while also working with Christian groups and ministries in her spare time. In 1956, she felt the Lord telling her to "quit nursing and go heal them!" Leaving England, she landed in the United States in Philadelphia at Christmas time and was very homesick. From Philadelphia she went on to Phoenix, Arizona, to A. A. Allen's meetings where she met a missionary lady and helped with her work among the American Indians until the Lord took the missionary home to glory.

In 1959, my mother's sister and husband, Auntie Barbara and Uncle Charlie, both took ill and died within three days of each other. When I wrote Barbara concerning their deaths and also of our parents' failing health, she quit her nursing job in Arizona, sold her trailer, and sailed home on the Queen Elizabeth II.

Upon returning to England, Barbara and a young evangelist held several weeks of meetings in an old cinema in Kingston, Herefordshire. She then helped conduct a three week tent revival in Wolverhampton with evangelist Alan Ball and Pastor Shaw. Pouring out His Spirit on both these endeavors, God greatly blessed with many healings and miracles. Following the tent revival, Barbara spent the next six months in Northern Ireland, for the first time holding meetings on her own.

Also while in England, Barbara ministered for a time at Headley Heath, and saw many young people's lives changed. One of the fellows who was saved in the meetings couldn't wait to get baptized in water. He came to us and said, "I've been down to the river and stood on the bank and said, 'In the name of the Father, Son, and Holy Ghost…' — and plunged in!"

For six months, between the passing of our mother in April 1961 and our father in October, Barbara preached every weekend at Hockley Pentecostal Church in Birmingham. The pastors, Miss Harriet Fisher and Miss Olive Reeve, who pioneered and built the church were two great women of God. They never took a salary or an offering, but had only a collection box in the back of the church. People could give if they wished, and these ladies never lacked!

These two sisters took Barbara and me under their wing at a very difficult time in our lives. Barbara was just in the beginnings of her ministry then, and they greatly encouraged us. Miss Fisher danced during all of our songs, and I said to Barbara, "I never saw anyone dance to a solo or a duet before!" Barbara replied, "I wouldn't care if they were standing on their hands!"

It was during this time at Hockley that Barbara's preaching ministry began to blossom. The Lord wonderfully blessed and gave us a great visitation, tripling the size of their congregation. I believe God gave us that tremendous harvest for the labor of our late parents.

In 1962, Barbara and I flew to Canada for the first time. When we arrived in the Toronto airport, there was no one to meet us. We waited until we were the only two left; the airport was empty and everyone was gone. Looking down at our suitcases, I said to Barbara, "I feel like a little orphan."

"Well, so we are!" she said, "Come on, let's get going."

"Where are we going?" I asked.

"We'll get a bus."

"Where to?" I asked again.

"To the YWCA!"

We jumped on the bus and off we went. The "Y" was full; but they gave us a little bed in the maid's quarters, where they kept the brooms and dusting material. We were so tired that when we got into the little bed, we soon fell asleep.

Opening the closet door in the morning, the startled maid exclaimed, "Oh! My goodness!" and quickly shut the door. I called to her, "It's all right, we'll be up in a minute." No one had told her we were there.

On Sunday we went to an Apostolic Church where the minister knew us and gave us a great welcome. We sang and Barbara spoke. A couple who had been our neighbors in Glasgow were in the congregation, and they invited us to their home and gave us accommodations. When my holiday time was over, I returned to England, but Barbara stayed and ministered in many churches around Ontario. This was the beginning of Barbara's ministry in Canada.

In her Christmas letter of that year she wrote:

> "The summer of this year was spent in meetings across Canada: preaching in churches in Ontario, Saskatchewan, Alberta, and British Columbia. The hand of the Lord was heavy upon me, and His power manifested in healings, restoration and deliverance. Also, I am ever thankful to God for His protection on the highways, trains, and airways.
>
> "When going west, I went out of my way to get off the plane at certain areas to visit great men who had been in the "Latter Rain" outpouring. I tried to get off at Banff in Alberta, but the people in the airport told me it would be very difficult. I asked, "Why would it be hard for me to get off in Banff, since that is where I want to go?" They answered, "Well, we've got an airport in Calgary, but don't have anything in Banff. Would you like a parachute?"

The son of the minister in Banff had a church in British Columbia, and Barbara was asked to go there and preach. She was also on a radio broadcast in Banff, after which a man phoned to ask if she was that girl from Scotland whose father had a church in Glasgow? It seems that nearing the end of the war, he had visited our home in Glasgow. Also, the wife of the pastor in Banff had been in our father's church in Glasgow. Recognizing Barbara, she said, "You've got the Massie 'look'!"

Barbara returned to England in the fall and concentrated her ministry in London and Birmingham. Before the Christmas holiday, she went to Holland and the Lord opened many churches in various cities for her to speak.

In June of 1963, Barbara and I flew back to Canada on a chartered flight from Belfast. I had to return home, but Barbara went on to Detroit and then to Florida.

In the fall of 1963, at a Full Gospel Businessmen's Conference in Florida, Barbara felt the drawing of the Spirit to go to the city of Oakland, California. Leaving the conference in a car given to her by friends with whom she was staying, she started out for Oakland with a stop-over in Houston, Texas.

Through an unusual set of circumstances in Houston, she was introduced to an Irish pastor, Gordon McGee, who had pastored in Belfast before coming to the USA. Having previously heard of Barbara, he asked if she would come and hold a meeting in his church. That one meeting turned into an eight week revival, continuing on through the Christmas season and into January of 1964. Barbara was usually very faithful to write home, but all during that time, we never heard from her! Not knowing she was going night and day in a visitation of the Spirit, we wondered whatever had happened to her and were concerned for her safety!

In February, she contacted the folks in Oakland that she was finally coming, and they cancelled all their speakers for the next six weeks. Before preaching in the morning meeting, the pastor told Barbara of a lady in the church who had been fasting for forty days, just finishing her fast that day. Fasting has a powerful effect of tearing down the enemy over a city and releasing the move of the Spirit of God; thus, from the very first meeting, the Lord poured out the wine and oil, and brought great rejoicing to the people. Over the weeks, pastors and ministers came from all around into that place, were touched by the Spirit, and took the blessing of God back to their own churches. Barbara always felt it was because of the faithfulness of that little woman to fast that the Lord had drawn her to that particular church in Oakland; and because of that little woman's faithfulness, the whole body of Christ in that area was blessed!

Shortly after sailing home in August 1964, Barbara received a letter from Holland asking her to take over a children's work in Hilversum. The children's evangelist, Tiny Stapersma, was preparing to go to America for a rest and needed someone to take over her flat and care for the work while she was away. Bella, Barbara's interpreter from previous visits to Holland, informed her that Tiny felt the Lord pressing her to ask Barbara to come and had inquired of a local minister concerning her. She thought the minister's answer was priceless: "She preaches like a red Indian!" he said. Barbara wondered if it was because she always wore feathers in her hats, but Bella said it was because she shouted out and maybe squawked too loud! After praying about the call, Barbara started packing her cases again and left in a few days for Holland.

When I arrived in Holland for a visit and saw Barbara with all of those children around her, I thought of the nursery rhyme, "There was an old woman who lived in a shoe. She had so many children, she didn't know what to do!" During her year in Holland, doors on every hand opened to Barbara. On the weekends she was free to minister in area churches where the power of God fell so mightily at times that folks often didn't know what hit them!

After her stay in Holland, Barbara and I flew back to Canada and the United States. In July 1965, we stopped at the summer camp meeting at Elim Bible Institute in Lima, New York and attended a 6 a.m. prayer meeting. At the end of the prayer time, Barbara saw a man for whom she felt led to pray. After giving him a prophetic word, she asked his name; he introduced himself as Wade Taylor, a teacher at the Bible school.

For the next year and a half Barbara preached in London, Haliburton, Kitchener, and for an extended time in Allsaw, Ontario until January 1967. In mid January, Barbara, very sick with pleurisy, arrived at 2 a.m. at some friends home in Rochester, New York. Her third day there the Lord gave her the text from Hosea 6:2, "After two days will He revive us: in the third day He will raise us up, and we shall live in His sight." On that third day, the Lord instantly healed her.

The friends with whom she was staying were going to Elim for Sunday morning worship and asked if she would like to come. When she walked into the school, she again met Wade Taylor who asked her to stay and speak that night. For the next several weeks, Barbara spoke and ministered in the Sunday chapel services. During those weeks God gave a mighty visitation of His Spirit, as His presence and anointing enveloped the school, filling the dorms, hallways, and classrooms, leaving an indelible mark on the lives of the students.

In a note Barbara later sent home, she wrote:

> "There was a real visitation in Elim Bible College, New York, while I was ministering there during the first term this year. I arrived mid-January and did not leave until Easter. The move of God on the lives of these students was something I'll never forget. The praise belongs entirely to the Lord — for of ourselves we can do nothing."

During the summer and fall of 1967, Barbara ministered in churches in New York, Pennsylvania, Michigan and Indiana. She also writes in her note, "While I was ministering in a large church in Benton Harbor, Michigan, I was privileged to become acquainted with the revival that is taking place in the Roman Catholic University of Notre Dame..." At the conclusion of an evening meeting, a nun from the University invited Barbara to drive back to the convent with them to minister in their 11:00 p.m. prayer meeting. The charismatic revival was new and fresh, and prayer meetings were being held continually around the campus, as priests, nuns and students were seeking God for the baptism in the Holy Spirit. Barbara was one of the first non-Catholics to go into Notre Dame and bring the blessing and anointing of the Spirit to them.

In 1970, Barbara first visited Pinecrest Bible Training Center in Salisbury Center, New York, where for many years, God gave her a wonderful ministry to the students. Pinecrest became her home and base while in the United States. For over twenty years as she traveled out from the school, the river of God's Spirit flowed mightily through her preaching and prophetic ministry, transforming many, many lives.

Each year for twenty-five years, I went to the States for my holidays. Barbara and I ministered together in many places in Pennsylvania, New York and New Jersey, as well as Canada. In 1982, we went to Jamaica and Haiti where the needs were tremendous. The people, especially in Haiti, were very poor and needed much prayer and healing.

In 1984, Barbara's friends in America honored her with a special banquet hosted by Pastor Tony D'Onofrio in Deer Park, Long Island, New York. There she was presented with a beautiful wristwatch, which she treasured. It was attended by many students, pastors and friends who had been blessed and healed through her ministry. At the end of the banquet, Brother Wade Taylor gave Barbara a prophetic word, saying the Lord was going to give her a fresh anointing. That word was fulfilled the very next day when a call came from a family we knew asking Barbara to come and pray for the husband's brother who was dying in Florida. The brother had undergone triple by-pass surgery and was given no hope. Barbara flew out the next day, ministered to the man, and the Lord healed him.

When we visited our sister Margaret in New Zealand in 1990, Barbara was not well. I could see the years of commitment and self-sacrifice in the Lord's work, especially the hot summers and severe winters in the United States, and all the driving alone on the big highways, had taken their toll on her health. Someone said to her, "Are you not afraid driving alone? Why don't you carry a gun?" She told them, "I carry my Bible and the Lord takes care of me!"

Barbara came home to Stafford in 1993. A severe stroke in November '94 saw her hospitalized and in a deep coma. Amazingly, she came round on Thanksgiving

Day and was heard whispering my name before slipping back to unconsciousness.

Barbara received her call home on December 15, 1994 following a second major stroke. Surely it is something more than coincidence that the date of her passing was exactly the same day she first went to the United States in obedience to God's call, some thirty-eight years before.

I was present with her as she passed from this life into life eternal. Declining the nursing staff's offer to call in a minister to Barbara's bedside, I knew it was proper that I should be the one to pray with and minister to her. As I stood beside her, the Lord clearly spoke within my spirit, "O death, where is thy sting? O grave, where is thy victory?" As His Word came to me, all my anxiety left, and such a sense of peace and release filled the room as Barbara's spirit entered into Paradise. Stepping outside the hospital, I looked up and saw the most perfect and radiant rainbow arching across our old market town of Stafford, even though there was no rain. I knew in my heart it was there to confirm the Word He had spoken to me at Barbara's bedside.

My heart filled with calm assurance, I went home and, switching on the radio, was greeted with the glorious refrains of the "Hallelujah Chorus" from Handel's "Messiah." For me, this set the final seal of victory and triumph on Barbara's departure, while at the same time reflecting a sense of the wonder and splendor of Barbara being welcomed into the presence of our Lord.

Sometime later, among her papers, I found a beautiful picture-card with the following scripture reference and poem:

"Then Shall I Know"
(I Cor. 13:12)

Not till the loom is silent
And the shuttles cease to fly
Will God unroll the canvas
And explain the reasons why
The dark threads are as needful
In the **Weaver's** skilful hands
As the threads of gold and silver
In the pattern **He** has planned.

A most apt and fitting epitaph for one whom the Lord called and equipped into His service as an evangelist, teacher, healer, and carrier of His anointing. Barbara's response to God's call contained no "why's," but rather a confidence built on entrusting her life into His hands. Now she, too, "shall know," along with the great cloud of witnesses, how right it was to take Him at His Word and stand secure on His promises.

Anne Massie
Stafford, England

<u>The Massie Family</u>: Aberdeen, Scotland
seated: Margaret, Willie, William W.
standing: Margaret, Anne, Barbara

Part Two

Barbara: Nursing Training School in Glasgow, Scotland.

We begin Barbara Massie's story with portions of her personal testimony taken from a message spoken at Elim Bible Institute in January 1967. In this message, Barbara brings us into her life at the time of God's calling upon her, taking her from her hometown and her nursing profession, and into Bible school.

From taped recordings, we have chronicled experiences which shaped her life and ministry from Bible school in South Wales in 1950 through the formative years of her ministry. These include the development of her preaching and prophetic word; then later her baptism in the new wine in Devon, England and in Holland in 1962.

Barbara's ministry was not born overnight; and this brief account shows how God orchestrated events and circumstances in her life to bring her into the fulness of His purposes and calling.

Barbara was one who was willing to pay the price for an anointed ministry. The dimension of the Spirit from which she lived and ministered is timeless and its principles unchanging. Her faith, trust, and explicit obedience to God were keys which unlocked power and anointing and brought wonderful fulfillment of God's promises in her life.

O RIVER OF GOD

---

chorus: Oh, River of God, Flow down on me;
Oh, River of God, Flow out through me.
Oh, River of God, So full and free-
Oh, River of God, I come to Thee!

1. A River is flowing from heaven above;
A River of blessing, A River of love.
'Tis reaching the Nations, both far and near
This River of God, Oh, let it flow here.

2. The deserts shall blossom, as fresh as a rose
This river brings healing wherever it flows
The ground that is parch'ed, so thirsty and dry,
Shall surely be flooded with rain from on high.

3. The fetters of fear and of doubt soon shall break,
When unbelief goes then the church shall awake.
The chains of hard bondage forever will fall-
And Jesus exalted, supreme over all.

4. The deaf shall have hearing, the blind folk shall see,
The lame shall be loosed from their infirmity.
The crooked made straight and the broken made whole;
This latter time blessing, as promised by Joel.

5. By this flowing River, earth's bondage shall cease
The floods are now rising to bring us release.
The vision is glorious, then why not believe;
And into this blessing, His promise receive.

Chorus Written in 1950 by James Beall Bethesda Missionary Temple
Detroit, Michigan
Verses Written in 1954 by Barbara Massie Stafford, England

The Mantle Of The Spirit Falls

Chapter 1

It took the river of God to change my life. I was serving God the best I knew how, doing all I could as God would give me strength and talent. But sometimes in the midst of service, God will call a halt; and in my experience, while serving God, I suddenly found dryness.

The children of Israel came out from the land of Egypt and as they were following the Lord, found themselves in a desert place. That was all right for the first month, but God never intended that they stay there wandering for forty years.

Sometimes in the will of God, when God brings us out from one experience and on our way into another, we suddenly find ourselves in an arid desert. Through no fault of our own (that we can put our finger on anyway), we find ourselves in a dry and barren place where we thought there should be streams and rivers; and so it was in my life.

After I had gone through all my training as a nurse and had risen to the top of the professional world, God said, "Come out from there and go into Bible school." I didn't intend on being a preacher; I thought maybe I'd be a missionary or something. I just didn't know what the Lord wanted! But I had a feeling that something was coming; I just couldn't put my finger on it. Thus, on the strength of God's word in my heart, I obeyed and went to Bible school.

The summer before I went into the Bible school in South Wales, I heard the principal preach a message that knowledge is power. Believing that, I left my profession; I left everything and went into school. After twelve months my heart was broken. I received a lot of head knowledge and knowledge of the Word, but my spirit felt empty. For deep down in my heart, I was passing through a wilderness way.

God had sent many things into my life to break my heart (and God will break your heart if He's going to use you). If your heart has never been broken, if you have never known brokenness in your life, you will never be bread! Corn used to make bread, the Bible says, must be broken; for it's bruised corn that is used to feed human kind. Before you can be bread for those who are hungry and water for those who are thirsty, there must be brokenness in your life.

Now the way that God took me may not necessarily be the way God will take you. Usually everything I started I finished. Being a preacher's daughter, we didn't have finances to send me to a higher school. Later, I did it the hard way; I put myself through nursing school. But, what broke my heart was I could not finish Bible school.

There was a deep hunger in my heart for the spiritual things of God, although I couldn't put a finger exactly on what it was I wanted. (I know now what I wanted because it's history—and I got what I wanted—but then, I didn't know.)

After one year God closed the door in South Wales where I was attending Bible school during the week and doing a nursing job on weekends. The job kept me rolling financially, but now that door closed. It seemed to be the leading of the Spirit that I wasn't to go back to Bible school; and I wanted to go back! Going down on my knees before the Lord but not receiving an answer from Him, I returned home and went back to my profession. However, the hand of the Lord was upon me, and for six months, though I couldn't explain why, I always wanted to weep and cry before the Lord.

We would come into prayer meetings and start praying, but it wouldn't be just praying. I would feel a rending deep within and begin to cry and cry. My father would say, "For goodness sakes, don't cry like that! The folks will think we're being hard on you or something!" He was the pastor, but he didn't understand what this was.

I was in this strange experience—and I wasn't the "weepy" kind. I would have been ashamed to let anybody see me weep. Even as a child if I fell, I wouldn't cry (maybe afterward when there was no one there); but I wouldn't cry for anybody, no matter how bad I felt. That's a stubborn Scot for you! But God was doing something different in my life. Sometimes in the services the tears would be rolling down my cheeks and I couldn't stop them—I got past being ashamed. And this didn't happen for just a day or a month, but went on for six months.

Then God arranged for me to go back to the school in the spring to be in what we called a reunion for the former students. Driving to South Wales on the 26th of May, 1951, I was the only one of the second year who came back. The others didn't bother, and I lived the farthest away.

Four brethren sent out by our church had immigrated to Canada and the States. Experiencing the latter rain visitation of God, three of them now returned and were ministering around the area. Fred Poole from Philadelphia was one of them. Up to that time there had been prophetic words given in the church, but never directed to a personal need. Through these men, for the first time, we knew what it was to have individual ministry. I didn't realize it, but God was getting ready to open the heavens and speak! My life would be changed forever!

These brethren were ministering at the Apostolic Temple just down the road from the school, and we heard that things were happening there. After our meeting at the school was over, we walked to the temple where they were ministering; and I saw things happening. There was a row of twenty-five or thirty people up front who had been seeking the baptism of the Spirit for ten, twenty, thirty and forty years. Real chronics I called them. I never thought they'd ever receive—neither did they. That's why they didn't!

Pastor Poole was walking down the line of people and talking to them quietly. I couldn't hear; so I crept up closer until I could hear what he was saying. He was telling them that it was their lips, their tongues, their mouths that would be speaking the glory of God; and to just lift their hands and begin to praise God.

As he touched the first one I said to myself, "He's got the most difficult one up there!" He put his hands on her, and when she opened her mouth and began to speak in tongues, I nearly fell over! For the first time in her life she began to speak the praises of God in another language! Then down the line he went, not missing a one. Each person received the baptism just like starting a car that had all its points and plugs ready to fire. A row of deaf people also suddenly received their healing.

As I saw God beginning to move in a new way, I began to feel deep down in my heart this was the "something" I had been trying to seek and to find—a fulfillment of what God was saying. Not just a doctrine or a ritual, not just a head full of knowledge; but the working power of God operating through lives—the anointing upon men and women that would break every yoke. I looked and I couldn't quite put a finger on it, or say just what it was—***but what they had I wanted!***

These men had known me through my father and some of them had stayed in our home when they were first preaching. Asking if I was there for the weekend, they invited me to attend the class they were speaking in the next day. I was thrilled! The next morning I went to the class, but without a hat! (Now in England, it was considered "proper" for women to wear hats in church.)

The class was held in a big student lounge, and Fred Poole was speaking. I was the only girl there. He told us about the visitation that started in Saskatchewan, Canada, and then spread down to Detroit and Philadelphia. He spoke of revival taking place in the churches day and night, and of people falling on their faces before the Lord as the Holy Spirit would minister. He gave us first hand news of what God was doing in America, and what God had done in his own heart. While he was speaking, I noticed some in the lounge turning around in their chairs, getting down on their knees and beginning to cry. I had tears in my eyes, but was trying to hide it! The Spirit of God was now dealing with ***us.*** Some in the room began falling off their seats like as if in agony. Pastor Poole just went on talking about the visitation. He knew what was happening to us; he knew the Spirit of the Lord had come in!

When I could sit no longer, I dropped to my knees beside my chair. I was ashamed: my eyes and nose were running, and I couldn't stop it—any more than I could stop it before! Some people turned their faces to the wall;

some went on the floor, and some went under the table or under their chairs. It was a weeping you couldn't stop and you couldn't explain. God was dealing with every life in that room and every life would be changed, absolutely transformed!

The former president of the Bible school was a very holy man. (During my first year, it was in his class I first felt the presence of God.) Suddenly realizing a woman was present, he came over to me, shook out his big white handkerchief and draped it over my head, making sure I would be in order when the Spirit of God began moving. So there I was: tears streaming down my cheeks, nose running, and a handkerchief over my head! I turned my seat to the wall for I didn't want anyone to see the mess I was in. Thinking of the handkerchief on my head, I took it off, wiped my tears, and blew my nose into the president's handkerchief!

It seemed every time man would come in with their traditions, the Lord would give me wisdom. That thing on my head had a use; so I put it to use! I tell you, when the Spirit of God comes down, you forget all about the old order. When you get off your feet, humble yourself before God and lay on your face before Him, you are in God's order, not man's. He says, "Humble yourselves under the mighty hand of God, and He will raise you up!"

During that meeting in the lounge, a young man from London who usually didn't prophesy opened his mouth and said, "Thus saith the Lord..." The word was that the students were to kneel down at a certain place and the brethren were to lay hands on them! The Lord said, "Be not afraid to do it, because some are ready and some are not. I will have those that are ready!"

Pastor Poole responded by saying, "We don't suddenly lay hands on anybody. The Bible says not to, and we normally don't; but this time the Lord has declared it and I feel a witness. So, when you feel ready, come and kneel at the chair and we will pray."

A chair was placed in the middle of the room, but no one moved; everyone was in their corner weeping. The fear of God was in that place and the weight of His presence was tremendous. Gradually, after a long spell, as we felt ready, we came and knelt by the chair; and the brethren gathered round and prayed.

Because they had said there ought to be preparation first (prayer and fasting), they hesitantly put their hands upon us in obedience to the prophetic word. But, you see, man doesn't know everything. Without realizing it, God had been preparing my heart for months—and God ***will come*** upon prepared hearts! When the way seems hard and barren and you feel you want to be doing something, but you don't know what it is or where to start, it is God the Holy Spirit working within you until the hour comes when the heavens open and everything that was a maze and darkness suddenly becomes very clear!

Eventually it was my time and I went up to be ministered to – weeping. I was trying to hold myself together and trying not to weep so I could hear what God was saying. The prophets gathered round and prayed, and God spoke to me through Pastor Poole, who was the prophet.

As the prophetic word came, I felt a mantle fall down upon me. I had never heard anybody preach on mantles, but I felt it come all over me. I knew then that whatever I did – whether I went on with God or went back – I knew I would never be the same again. I might be ten times better; I might be a hundred times worse because of my own way, but I could not be the same. And I believe that anybody who has felt the flick of the mantle of our Great Elijah will never be the same again. If you have felt the touch of that mantle, you can't turn back! You will go on for God!

Out of seventeen students in the room that day, the Lord spoke prophetically to only three or four of us; and I was one of them! I couldn't believe what the Lord was saying: He told me He was giving me one gift!

Because I was a nurse, I thought I would have liked a healing ministry. Since I was a child, any old dog or cat that came along with a limb that needed to be bound up, I'd tie it up and try to help it. All of my life I had been nursing people, and I said, "Lord, why don't you give me a healing ministry?" These thoughts were in my mind as I was listening to what God was saying. Then Pastor Poole said to me, "The word of wisdom will be found in your mouth and the word of knowledge!"

As the word of the Lord came upon others, I listened and heard God say He was giving ***them*** the ministry of healing and the gift of miracles! And I felt God had forgotten me! But over the years, I watched many who had been given these gifts later become unwilling or tripped up by something, and they lost out with God. However, I found that as I walked along in the wisdom, knowledge and understanding that God was giving me, all these signs were following anyway. God said He would give me wisdom; and with wisdom, He gave me all those other gifts as well! I needn't have worried! God was faithful to His Word!

The Spirit of God came upon my life there in that student lounge, and I was anointed after all that struggle! God took up then what I had learned in Bible school and began to show me truth that before seemed so difficult to grasp.

When the mantle of the Spirit came upon me, the Holy Spirit led me into His Word and opened up my understanding and I received truth in my heart and spirit that I will never forget. For when the Holy Spirit quickens His Word, or suddenly lights upon a word that somebody speaks, you will never lose that thought; you will never lose that truth. And so God broke into my life!

That morning while crying somewhere in a corner of the lounge, I remembered another time twelve months before when, as a student, I had been kneeling in prayer. Each morning at seven, the students came to the lounge and prayed for a half an hour to an hour. Some students slept and some prayed. The next day another group would sleep and the rest would pray.

On one of those mornings, the Spirit of God came upon me as I prayed and I said, "Lord, we need a milestone... we need somewhere we can say, 'Here I met God.' Like Jacob when he said, 'This is my Bethel: right here!'"

That morning I thought, "Dear God, I need a place where I can say, 'I have met You!'" I then left school without having that milestone. Now, twelve months later, I was back to that same place, perhaps even the same chair. However, it wasn't until they were calling us to kneel that I suddenly realized God's answer. This was the fulfillment of that which I had asked the Lord twelve months before. I had forgotten all about it, but the Lord does not forget! That is how important our prayers are.

Therefore, ***believe God*** for fulfillment: don't ask small, ask big… ask largely and believe God for the answer and you will get it!

I Believe God

Chapter 2

At the close of the weekend reunion in Wales, we attended one last service. The young man who was preaching that night was a third year student. ***"I believe God!"*** was his message. As he was preaching, those of us on the platform with him all began to groan and cry as the Holy Spirit was moving upon us in prayer and weeping. He had not been in the lounge earlier when the power of God had fallen, and he didn't realize that God was sweeping into this meeting in a new way. Neither did the people in the audience know what was happening, and I'm not sure I knew myself; but there was a burning and groaning in our spirits.

Crying out to God, we slipped off our seats and onto the floor. Soon the preacher couldn't be heard over the groans from around his feet. But he kept saying, ***"And I believe God; I believe God*** !" I had heard these words, ***"I believe God "*** many, many times before. But that night they seared right into my heart. Those words became like a branding iron and burned deep into my spirit. Oh, how much they meant to me, and I laid hold upon them. God gave me those three words that night as a gift.

The next morning, as I left where I was staying and went down to the school to say goodbye, I had such a fear in my heart about leaving. In the past, I had come out of meetings and conventions greatly blessed and full of fire; however, before long, I always lost the blessing!

When I came down from the mountain top, that stirring would go away. I wondered if it would be the same this time; and I felt deeply troubled.

Walking into the school, I saw the students not in their classes; but all around the piano singing, dancing and praising God— and I felt worse. Inside I was quietly crying, yet rejoicing too. Though feeling the warmth and the glow of all of this, I still had the thought: "What am I going to do? They are all here, and I am going away!"

The principal's wife came up to me and said, "Oh, I'm so glad you came by, Sister Barbara. I had a dream in the night and I just asked the Lord to send you by so I could tell you about it. It will encourage you." She said, "I saw the school as a tree of glory. The branches were like sparks going out from the tree, and there were names on the sparks. Then, I saw one spark, a very bright one, come off the tree. It went the farthest of any of the sparks, and your name was on it!" She said, "I thought I would tell you because I have a feeling you don't really want to go home." I replied, "No, I don't; but I have to go back to Stafford and run the hospital. I am second in command!"

Still, I could not stop thinking, "What chance do I have?" I was remembering the blessings in past meetings and conventions, times when some of the cream of the ministry came from the ends of the earth to minister. We would all be uplifted and feeling great, even as young as we were. Then little by little, we would lose out! Our bottles would leak. I was so afraid this would happen again, and I didn't want to lose what I had received. Then the Lord gave me this text in John's epistle, "The ***anointing*** I have given you, will ***abide*** with you forever!" (I John 2:27) When God quickened this verse to my heart, I knew I had heard from heaven!

As I drove back from the Bible school in Penygroes, South Wales to Stafford, England, the Presence of the Lord was with me in the car and He spoke to me all the way home. I was so utterly astonished at what He was telling me that I never saw a stop sign or a traffic light; I was not aware of the road or the journey. I just drove straight through Wales and the first thing I remember seeing was the sign for Stafford. In amazement, I thought, "This is a four hour drive and here I am!" I was home in record time!

One of the things the Lord told me was He wanted me to preach Thursday night — the very first meeting after coming home! I never wanted to preach; I always liked somebody else up doing that! Even in Bible school, I would get one of the fellows to take my turn, as they always seemed eager to speak. But the Lord said, "You must do it!" When I heard what He was saying to me, I bowed to His will. As the day drew near, I grew sick with worry. But in my heart were these three words: "***I believe God!***"

Barbara: Assistant Matron in charge of the Hospital in Stafford.

Anne and Barbara in Glasgow, Scotland.

Thursday Night

Chapter 3

I returned from Wales under the power of the Spirit and the minute I stepped out of the car, I lost all desire for food and began to fast and pray. That Thursday morning, I was in charge of the maternity section of the hospital and was the only midwife on duty.

In this section were five women all with brand new babies. One woman who just had her first baby called me over, indicating she wanted to talk with me privately. It was morning, and thinking something might be wrong, I leaned over and she whispered in my ear, "I've got something to tell you! While nursing my baby this morning and looking out across the room, I saw something."

"What did you see?" I asked.

"Up on the wall," she continued, "I saw a Middle Eastern vessel, like you see in faraway places. It had a handle on it. And while I was nursing the baby and looking, a hand took this vessel, tipped it over, and out came a whole lot of water."

At that moment my heart began to sing because this was the day I was to speak! I said to her, "Then, what happened?"

"It just went away!" she replied.

Inside I was saying, "Hallelujah! Praise the Lord! This is the day! To an unsaved woman, the Lord has shown that the water of His Spirit will be poured out!"

Leaning over her as she was still talking, she asked, "Does this always happen with the first baby?"

"Oh, Yes!" I answered. "They often see jugs of water on the walls!" With that, her fear was pacified and my fear was gone. I knew; I just knew!

When the Lord told me I was to speak Thursday night, I didn't tell anyone. When God lets you know something, you don't have to try to work it out and make it easy for the Lord! Nobody knew I would be speaking, except for the phone calls I made telling people to come to the service because God was about to visit Stafford with revival. In my heart, I was saying, "***I believe God!***

By Wednesday night my father was very upset with me, warning me that if I lifted that phone to call any more people, he was canceling the meeting. He said, "I don't know what has gotten into you!" I assured him that something ***was*** going to happen; and he assured me that I was out of my mind! He was the pastor, but I was calling for everyone to come when as yet there was no sign of rain, not even a little cloud in the sky. The first sign I received was from this little woman who saw the jug of water on the wall!

The man scheduled to speak that night was someone who would speak "no matter what!" If something happened that he couldn't, the overseer was next in line. Arriving early to the meeting, I walked up to the overseer and asked him if he had heard from God that day. His reply was, "No," but he quickly changed it to, "Yes! I hear everyday!" I knew his first answer was the right one.

As I sat down by the piano, my eyes were all red from crying. In my own private room in the hospital, while still in uniform, I had been kneeling by my bed crying like a baby — this was all too much for me! I didn't want to speak, but I knew I had to. I knew the Lord wanted me to go in and make a way for Him where there was no way. I said, "Lord, I can't do it; I don't even know what to say!" He impressed upon me to start by giving my testimony.

When the meeting was about to begin, I was thinking, "No one has asked me to speak, Lord. If you don't open the way… I am not pushing…" Just then the door opened, and a young man came flying up the aisle. Addressing me, he said, "My cousin, who is the speaker tonight, can't come. His wife is deathly ill; they think she's dying and he has gone with her in the ambulance to the hospital." Then he said, "We heard by phone that you have been in Wales and the latter rain is falling, and you are in it. Would you tell us about it?"

"Sure," I answered, "but you have to clear it with the overseer." Hearing the news, the overseer said, "All right then. She can do that!" And suddenly I realized, "I ***am*** speaking!" The Lord opened the way for me that night, and I stood up and began to tell what had happened in Penygroes and how the Lord was moving. His Word was burning in my heart!

God had promised me revival and visitation that night. It was a May evening and still light outside when I got up to speak. The hall was bright, so no one put the lights on. As I was speaking, it began getting dark; but still no one got up to put the lights on, and we were not able to see much after a while. The devil whispered in my ear: "Nothing is going to happen!" But I kept on speaking. When you have cut the moorings and are out from the shore, there is no turning back!

In the fading light, I was finding great freedom in preaching to faces I couldn't see! Finally, losing all my fear, I began to get caught up in what I was saying and went on from my testimony to tell other things. When I finished, it seemed as though nothing was happening — except that I was speaking — which was really something new! Before I went to my seat, I spoke these three words — I shouted them out — ***"I believe God!"***

At that the overseer shot up and said, "Put the lights on! Time to go! Let's sing the doxology!" He tried to close the meeting, but no one was listening! In the darkness, not able to see people's faces, I had no idea of what was going on in the congregation. I wasn't aware that people were shaking under the power of God and falling from their seats, as the Spirit of God was moving all over the room.

As I stepped down, a crippled woman of about thirty-five stood up and began praising the Lord. She had been holding her hands up, and I thought she was praying for me. She spoke out, "I saw the Lord standing beside Sister Barbara; then He came to me, reached down and took my hands." For over three quarters of an hour her hands were raised, and I wondered why she wasn't getting tired; but the Lord was standing beside her holding her hands all that time! I didn't see Him, but I felt His Presence! Then she said, "Something is happening in my limbs; I can feel my legs straightening out!" Although previously she had received a partial healing, that night the Lord touched her anew and began to complete her healing.

After standing for quite a while, she sat down and said, "My servant that is on the floor, the Lord will deliver you this night!" Kneeling at my seat, I was not aware of anyone on the floor. As I looked through my fingers, I saw this young guy, who had been sitting at the back, now writhing on the floor. The power of God was there and that devil couldn't sit still in that fellow. It threw him to the floor and he was going through the seats like a snake. The Lord showed me that he had an unclean spirit.

I knew my father had the ministry of deliverance, but when he and the elders prayed, that devil would not budge. Several people said to me, "You go up, Barbara!" And I said, "No." I knew the Lord would give me the right time, for timing is very important in the work of the Lord. Somehow, I had already learned that there is a time for everything. (If we learn nothing else, we must learn to be on time and not run ahead of the Lord, because He is the One who gives miracles.)

Three times a prophetic word came that the Lord would deliver His servant that night. The third time, the Lord said to me, "Go, now!" I immediately went over, stretched my hands toward him, named that spirit, and at the first command it came out! The young man was instantly delivered and began to glorify God.

Now, it wasn't because of me that the deliverance came, but the Lord had prepared me. I knew certain spirits only came out by fasting and prayer. My father hadn't fasted, but I had, and the power of God came through fasting.

One miracle after another happened that night, and we had a tremendous move of the Spirit until the wee hours of the morning – the latter rain had come to Stafford! The name "Stafford" means a "stony place," but when revival came and remained, it became known as "the place of the rain" – and people came from all over to see!

That Thursday night was a new beginning in my ministry. The next day, the man's wife, who had fallen so sick before the service, mysteriously recovered and was sent home from the hospital. The doctors couldn't understand it, and no one knows till this day what had happened to her!

The Prophetic Gift And Beginning Ministry

Chapter 4

Many details led up to my moving in the realm of the prophetic. One significant experience occurred during my year in Bible school. Oftentimes throughout that year I would feel very much alone. In those times I would go to my room to seek the Lord, and He would be so close.

On this particular occasion while I was waiting on the Lord, kneeling and praying, His manifest Presence came into my room. There in His Presence I began to feel a strange warming coming deep within. Now, I was baptized in the Holy Spirit when I was fourteen or fifteen and I knew the presence of the Lord, but immediately I recognized this was something new and different.

Conscious of the Lord standing there, I waited to see what He would say to me. It seemed He was there to give me something, though I did not know what. All the while I was sensing this heat — a tremendous warmth and glow — like fire burning deep within.

Feeling like I wanted to do something, I stood up and walked around my room. As His Presence lifted, I had an excited feeling deep inside. (When you are in the power of the Spirit, sometimes that same feeling of warmth will come just before you speak.) I didn't realize it then, but the Lord visited me that day to give me the prophetic gift.

Two or three weeks after that experience, we were in a Sunday morning service in the little Welsh village where the Bible school was located. The custom of the church was to break bread every Sunday morning, and after partaking of the bread and wine, we would worship the Lord. It was understood this was not a time to make requests, but to praise the Lord for all He had done through Calvary and to make a fresh covenant with Him. One by one we would stand up and thank the Lord and worship Him by the Spirit.

This Sunday morning, while breaking bread and worshiping, I remember standing up to praise the Lord. As I was thanking and praising Him and saying the words that were coming to me, I was aware again of this strange heat and burning deep within.

One of the young fellows, who was in the school for a refresher course that year, came to me afterwards and said, "Can I walk down the road with you, Barbara?" "Sure!" I replied. He was recognized as a young "prophet" in the church.

As we walked down the road together he said, "Barbara, did you know that you have prophecy?" Startled by his question, I answered: "Brother, I would ***never*** say, 'Thus saith the Lord!' How could you say, 'Thus saith the Lord'? What if it wasn't the Lord? What would you do; wouldn't that be terrible?"

"But," he said, "I'm telling you! You're a prophet! Do you know you have stolen my prophecies for the last few weeks?"

"What do you mean?" I asked.

He continued, "When you got up and praised the Lord this morning, I was just about to give a prophecy; and you took it out of my mouth and gave it word for word. Then you said, 'Amen,' and sat down! That was prophecy you had!"

Well, I didn't know what to think about it all; so I went to my room. It was then I remembered that while worshiping the Lord in the service, that same warmth and glow was in my heart that came into my room when the Lord's Presence came! So I prayed and, like Mary, I hid that word in my heart, then asked the Lord to ***"hold fire!"*** Since I was the only girl in the Bible school in Wales, I was hesitant to begin prophesying there, and I asked the Lord to ***hold fire*** until I was back home with my own people. Then I would say, ***"Thus saith the Lord!"***

—∾—

Arriving home from our reunion in May, the first thing I did was to make a covenant with the Lord. I said, "Lord, if You will let that strange warming come back upon me when I'm here among my friends, if You will let that happen again, then I'll do it. If it kills me, I'll open my mouth and I'll do it!" (We will never get anywhere with God if we are not willing to be killed. We're no use to God until we are dead!)

I never did want to say, "Thus saith the Lord," for I was afraid. My mother had a great love for the word of the Lord and a great desire to hear the prophetic word. To her, the word was very precious! She raised us in a godly fear — not terror — but a godly fear of the word of the Lord. Therefore, none of us had any desire to say, "Thus saith the Lord," — because it was a holy thing. That word would carry life, or it would carry death!

I thought, "How could I know if it is, "Thus saith the Lord?" So I asked the Lord to give me certain signs and to let me feel the moving of His Spirit upon me. In the next Sunday afternoon prayer meeting, following Thursday night, the Lord fulfilled every sign. An altar call was made at the end of the prayer service, and a number of folks went up for prayer. Kneeling at the front, some were seeking healing and some the baptism in the Holy Spirit. As I looked down the row, a terrible weariness came over me, and I perceived by the Spirit that no one would receive anything. They had been prayed for so many times before.

As I looked at them, suddenly I felt the warm glow of the Spirit, His Word within me. Everyone was kneeling and I thought, "O God, You've taken me at my word; now, I must do it!" Don't ever lay a fleece with God and not obey Him. You might miss God by a mile or miss Him forever. God does not like disobedience. Looking around, I prayed, "Oh God, help me!"

As the Holy Spirit began to move within me, I opened my mouth and began to speak. All I did was open my mouth and begin to speak, for the Spirit gave the utterance. It wasn't stammering lips; it wasn't a few words here or there, but God the Holy Spirit came upon me. As I spoke, there issued forth a river of living water!

I have forgotten thousands of prophecies I have given, for it has nothing to do with my mind; but I will always remember this one because it burned in me before I gave it. It was such a struggle to open my mouth!

The Lord was moving upon me, and I began to say, ***"Thus Saith The Lord,"*** for the first time! The Lord said, "I have brought My people out from the land of Egypt and from the house of bondage. I have brought them out that I might bring them into the land of promise, not to have them wander in the wilderness, but to bring them in. Surely, surely I have delivered thee... Surely, I will fill thee... Surely, I will meet thy need..." The Lord told them they would receive healing and infilling.

When I finished prophesying, I hardly knew what hit me! I opened my eyes and everybody was on the floor. My mother was crying and weeping at the top of her voice. Everyone was crying. I don't remember all the Lord said, for it was not me! It was an invasion of the Holy Spirit! People were healed and filled with the Spirit all over the place, without tarrying, searching and waiting. The latter rain was falling, and it was time for receiving.

Just before I opened my mouth to give the prophetic word, the devil said to me, "It's only just a little bit of water! What ***is there*** in what you have? " I could feel the word coming; and I knew in my mind the sense of what God was going to say, but how it was to come, how it would be expressed, I did not know. Having an understanding of what God was about to say, the devil then said to me, "That's not very much! Surely somebody has said that before!" But, I carried the water until the time of the pouring forth.

As soon as the Spirit of God said to me, "Now! Now is the time!" I began to prophesy and something happened! As the water poured forth, it became wine. It just hit the floor all around and the Spirit of God invaded that place. God moved in, pouring out His Spirit like they had never seen before! The Spirit of God was so released that folks could not stay upright, but were falling from their seats as the Spirit of God came down like a weight of glory.

I had come home from that weekend in Wales full of the blessing of God. The anointing of the Holy Ghost had turned my life upside down; and within a week my church, my parents, and my home were turned upside down as well by the power of God!

A New Thing

Chapter 5

This fresh outpouring of God's Spirit was so strange and so new that everyone was on their faces before the Lord. My father exclaimed, "Everything is going haywire!" He had experienced revival in the past, but nothing like this. Why, though, should God always do things the same? Isaiah says, "Behold, I do a ***new thing!***"

Revival came to our church and from there it spread to many parts of England. It was a time of fullness, and the Holy Spirit was being poured out like a mighty river! Everyone was calling Stafford, England, where I came from, "the place of the rain" — and it was just me coming back after God had visited my life! To me this was all a miracle, for I never believed the Lord could ever use me to speak His word or to be a channel for the river of God to flow through in such blessing!

From this time on, my home and my church were turned upside down. My father would say to me, "You must behave yourself - you keep phoning everybody! How do you know what will happen on Sunday?" He had a big notice out in front of the church saying, "Meetings as usual on Sunday." I said to him, "You should change that!" He said, "I think I'll have to or else put you out!" The unusual was becoming the usual in the meetings.

Our denomination did not like women ministry, and my father said to me, "You're before your day. I don't know what we'll do with you!" Had it been my brother, they would have said, "Amen!" and made him an apostle or a prophet. However, they didn't know what to do with me! Whenever I opened my mouth, I was right out of order! If I were a man, I would probably have been a big shot in some church (and been killed dead with flattery). However, a little persecution and a little bit of knocking down causes one to lean upon the Lord!

There was one woman in our church in Stafford whose husband owned a garage. My father, being the pastor, didn't want to offend her! She was one of our best members and I really loved both her and her husband. I used to sit in the front and play one of those little pedal organs. Once, as she leaned over to someone, I heard her say, "It was so different before Barbara came back from that school. It used to be safe to invite neighbors or relatives in. Everything was decent and in order. We would sing hymns and then pray for the sick. Now, you don't know who might suddenly jump up and say, 'I'm healed! I can breathe! My lungs were tight, but now I can breathe!' Or someone else will just get up and say, 'Oh, my headache's gone.' And nobody had even prayed for them! Or someone else might start crying out loud, or laughing for nothing -- just start laughing. When you sit down, you don't know who might fall off their seats, or when the service will even end!"

In that hour God was sweeping through in a fresh new way. In the meetings, as the Spirit of God would pass by, it was too heavy for some and off their seats they went – and they did ***well*** on the floor! The revival brought in a new wave of God's Spirit, and with it a new movement of God.

It was when this latter rain blessing came to me, and the assurance of God's hand upon my life that I needed those three words," I ***believe God!"*** However, I didn't just sit and wait. Whenever I felt a need of strength to go someplace, or if I received a revelation or a "feeling" that God was about to do something, then I would begin to abstain from food!

Fasting was no sacrifice. When the burden would come upon me to stand in the gap for a meeting, then I would not be able to eat. Not feeling strong in myself, and not feeling like I was a great preacher who was adequate to go in and do the job, I leaned heavily upon the Lord and gave myself to prayer and fasting.

When people came into our home, they expected me to be the life of the conversation. Now, when the burden of the Lord came upon me, I would have nothing to say. Usually I would leave the room or would not be eating, and people would ask, "What happened to her?" Mother would just say, "Well, she's in a quiet spell!" As I was going up the stairs one time, I heard her say, "She's just in a quiet spell, and when she goes quiet, something is about to happen." In those times, it seemed like a separation would come upon me that would drive me into the Presence of God where the Lord would speak to me. And I assure you: I was not lonely! Before that, though, when people were downstairs, it was the hardest thing for me to go upstairs and pray; I would feel like a hermit.

After the Holy Spirit came upon me in 1951, I wanted to be before the Lord all the time. There is something about that upper chamber when the Spirit of God beckons you and God wants you before Him, that you must obey Him! Jeremiah says, "Seek ye the Lord, while He may be found; call upon Him while He is near."

I came into my ministry the hard way. You might not think that would be true since I was a preacher's daughter, but I was raised in religious tradition. I had to ***believe God,*** and that would put me right out there on a limb, wondering what on earth would happen next! It seemed that whenever the Spirit would begin to move, everybody sat back and just looked at me! They didn't know what was going to take place and I didn't either. But I was ready and willing.

Finding that I could be useful to the Lord became such a treasure to me. I might not have been everything that I could have been; but I know this, I was never the same after the word of the Lord came over me! And I don't know how many people - perhaps hundreds and hundreds - have been changed because ***I believed God,*** obeyed Him and said, ***"Thus Saith The Lord!"***

Chapter 6

Fred Poole and the brethren from the States, who brought the latter rain blessing to the Bible school in May 1951, were only in the country another two months. For those two months in whatever time I had off from my hospital job, I arranged to travel to where one of these men would be ministering, no matter how far it was.

For six weeks I never rested. In an afternoon or an evening that I had off, I crossed lakes, rivers and roads by car; I drove miles and miles to the nearest place where one of them was speaking. I felt an urgency upon me because I knew their time was short – and I was so hungry! Like a sponge, I absorbed everything they had to say; I drank in every word!

By now I was beginning to move out in God myself and, as I followed these brethren, I would be called out along with them to minister in the prophetic word and the laying on of hands. I didn't especially want to minister, but I would be obedient to do whatever the Lord would tell me to do. I was so happy to hear the voice of the Lord speaking to me, that I gladly obeyed!

However, before hands were laid on me I was bound by a spirit of fear. It wasn't demon possession or an evil thing, but it was a bondage, a shackle. I was afraid of people's faces and afraid to move. But when the word of the Lord came over me, it went like fire through me; and that spirit left! It was as if the Lord made me new all over again. He set me on the potter's wheel, and when I came off I was a different person! The Lord took away all of that fear, and He gave me a warning: He said, "I've got a big work for you to do; but if you disobey Me, I'll lift My anointing." Suddenly, I lost my fear of man, because I did not want to grieve the Lord. From then on, come what may, I would do whatever the Lord asked me to do. That fear of man was gone!

Through the summer months, the revival was going on in our church in Stafford. August 4th came and it was time for the big convention of the Apostolic Church in South Wales. Seven days before this convention, the Lord gave me a prophetic word to speak to the whole assembly. Those next seven days and nights I spent on my face, fasting and praying for the courage to go with the message God had given me. In our denomination women were not to prophesy; but I could not be silent. I knew I had to do what women, by tradition, were not to do, and it would upset their laws and doctrine. It would be my death and funeral, but I had to obey the Lord!

Owning a new car at that time, I drove with my mother and my sister, Anne, down to Penygroes. We stayed in a house about two miles from the conference, and when we went to get into the car to go to the meeting, it had a flat tire! The Lord impressed on my heart, "Taxi, Taxi!" "We'll get a taxi," I told my mother. The lady who owned the house said, "My brother owns a taxi, and does country taxi work. I'll call him." Since there was no telephone, someone ran down to get him. He came up and offered to fix the car, but I said, "No, we need a taxi!"

If we were to find a seat at the convention, I knew we had to be on time; I knew, too, that I must sit where my voice could be heard. We should have been there an hour early, but instead arrived only half an hour before the meeting began, and the orchestra had already started to play.

The building, holding two thousand, was already full. People were crowded into the doorways and no one else could get in. I said in my heart, "Lord, this is good! My burden will lift, and I won't have to do it!" Suddenly, a fellow turned around and said, "Oh, here are the Massie girls! Make way everybody. Make way." The people all stepped back and we were ushered in!

In the taxi on the way to the meeting, I made a covenant with the Lord that if my place in the orchestra were open, which would be a miracle, then I would do whatever He asked me. When we walked in, the orchestra section was already jammed full; and those who hadn't come early enough lost their seats. But there was one seat open at the end — where I always sat!

Not being able to walk past anyone to get to my seat, someone helped me over the side rail and let me down into the orchestra section. Suddenly, I saw Anne come flying over. Way in the back someone had given up his seat for her. But my seat was empty — an angel had been sitting in it and nobody else could! Instead of feeling brave, I went weak as water and was about to die; for I knew I was committed now and had to do it. I went all weak; I had no voice and I couldn't sing. I couldn't do a thing but just sit there!

While the offering was being taken, a song was sung about God's Word being as sure as a bank, or something along those lines. Later on, as the preacher was speaking and coming to the climax of a tremendous message, a man who could be a perfect nuisance suddenly stood up. He had been sitting and thinking about the offering; and now he jumped up and said, "God's bank is the best bank; yes, the best bank in the world!" And the whole congregation fell apart laughing! The speaker was so frustrated and devastated by the interruption that he couldn't go on.

This man got up again and said, "Lord, release Your key men and Your key women in this convention." (Key women - now that was most unusual!) "That Thy will may be done in this convention!" Immediately, the Spirit of the Lord spoke to me and said, "You are the key, only the key. Why are you anxious?"

Just that quickly, everything fell off me like chains. All the weakness and that watery feeling left, and I felt strong as a lion. The minute I stood up and opened my mouth to give the word of the Lord, God the Holy Spirit came in like a shaft of light. I've never seen anything like it before or since. He came in; and I became a different person. The fire began to burn, and there were people slain all over the place by the power of God. The word was along the lines of, "When I promised you bread, I wouldn't give you a stone! When I promised you fish, I wouldn't give you a serpent!"

As I gave the prophetic word, their whole program was upset. People began weeping throughout the congregation, and the leaders couldn't continue with their schedule. When I stood and said, "Thus saith the Lord," I came against all their traditions, for a woman wasn't to speak or to prophesy! All the rules were broken and all the shackles were broken. There was weeping all over the building. The loudest weeping, I found afterwards, was coming from the students from the Bible school -- the students I left behind when I had to go back to the Midlands and to my profession.

When the outpouring came in May, these students were so caught up in blessing they stopped classes for weeks. They did a lot of singing and praising, but then there came a kind of stalemate. The blessing eased a bit, and they went back to their studies and the classrooms. Later on they became distracted by troubles and problems, and without realizing it, they lost what God had given them. Instead of dwelling in the upper air, in the high places where God dwells, instead of going out and breaking forth upon others, they stagnated.

Now in this convention, when the Spirit of God moved through that place, they all swept right back into the latter rain experience. I am not referring to the "Latter Rain Movement," but the latter rain of the Spirit as spoken of in the Holy Scriptures. The students and the younger ministers of that organization came right back into the blessing of God.

Later that week, the older ones came to me and said, "We had this forty years ago. We've been through all this. This is nothing new!" My reply was, "What you had forty years ago didn't do me any good. I wasn't born yet, how could it help me? I have to have my own portion of the latter rain!"

While the students had stayed on at the school, I was thrust out alone. Even though I knew God was with me, it wasn't easy. Many times my heart was broken and I nearly gave up. At times opposition from religious traditions seemed more than I could take, but I never did stagnate! When you are in a battle, you don't stagnate. Because there were so many darts coming my way, I had to keep my armor bright, fighting all the time, fasting and praying and getting through to God.

Although I wanted to stay on in school, God meant for me to go out. But the Lord saw to it that being scattered did not mean I would lose the blessing. For had I stayed in school and experienced no opposition, where would I be? God wanted me to go out with the blessing, and thus the scattering became my life-saving!

THE APOSTOLIC TEMPLE, PENYGROES.

Philadelphia To Phoenix – Without Hats

Chapter 7

In 1956, on a word from the Lord, I left England and sailed to the United States. Coming to a strange country for the first time, and arriving in Philadelphia ten days before Christmas, was very difficult for me. I had visited Europe and other places, but only as a nurse doing a little traveling. This time I had left my own country, and it was really a trial. However, in Pastor Fred Poole's church in Philadelphia, which was a center for what God was doing at that time, I had opportunity to attend a number of meetings.

Before I came to America, God spoke to me: "quit nursing them and go heal them." He also put a word in my heart about going to Phoenix. I didn't even know what Phoenix was. At first I thought it had something to do with the Sphinx in Egypt. Then I thought it might be on the south coast of France or in Syria or Egypt somewhere. Looking at a world map, I saw that it was the state capital of Arizona. I then began making my plans with just this one word the Lord put in my heart – Phoenix! I also knew that I would stay there, living out of my own pocket, for I had sold my car and all my possessions. And I wasn't going to ask anybody for anything!

Upon arriving in Philadelphia, I went to a large convention where a number of representatives of the full gospel were ministering: Tommy Hicks, Gordon Lindsay and others (famous men that had only been names to me back in England). Also attending from Dallas, Texas, were evangelists M.A. and Jane Collins Daoud, who had a world-wide evangelism and miracle ministry; and I felt a great drawing to speak to them.

It was during this time the Lord spoke to me about giving a faith offering. In the meetings they were asking for faith pledges of one hundred dollars. I never heard of that before. To me it was the craziest thing to ask for a pledge. Being from England, we were respectable and didn't do that kind of thing. We were Pentecostal people and gave our tithes, but they wanted a pledge.

The Lord said to me, "Give it!" But I didn't have a hundred dollars, and I said to Him, "That's not right! If you say, 'I'll give a hundred dollars' and you don't have it; then that's not true." I didn't have a job and I didn't know where I was going next, but the Lord said, "Give it anyway!" He wanted to teach me about a faith offering and giving – giving even what you didn't have. It took me a week to learn that lesson.

This Scotsman fought for seven days; all through those meetings I fought. I would have given it if I had it, but I didn't have it. You see, the Lord wanted to take my faith up higher. But every time I would step up, I'd come back down. I wouldn't stay up there. When they would ask for a faith pledge, I would raise my hand up just so far and then pull it back down again.

On the seventh day I was still tormented about that pledge. When I arrived at the meeting, the man was saying, "Hundred dollar pledges, now." Instantly, my hand shot up while I was still walking to my seat. He waited until I sat down, and said, "We are calling now about the hundred dollar pledges." And up went my hand again.

I had been trying all week not to do that, but now I couldn't keep my hand down. The man probably thought I was a bit off and didn't know what I was doing. So for the third time he said, "We are talking about pledges for the mission work for the Italian churches. We want hundred dollar pledges." Up went my hand. In fact, I put up two hands so he would know. I'm sure he thought I was a bit of a nut!

All this time I was wanting to meet the Daouds and speak with them, but everyday there would be a crowd of people around them. I didn't know that in America you just push in. I was trying to be polite, and I couldn't get near them. However, just at the moment I signed that card at the front for the hundred dollars, the Daouds came over and I was introduced to them.

In our conversation they asked if I would like to go to Dallas with them. I said, "I sure would, but I'm not going to Dallas. I am going to Phoenix!"

"Well," they said, "that's funny; we're going to Phoenix too. But we first must go to Dallas to get our magazine out. Would you like to come?" I said, "Sure, but I ought to pray about it."

Taking my New Testament into a little corner of the building I prayed, "Lord, I'm in a stew and don't know what to do. Is there anything in this Book that will tell me, a Scotsman away from home, whether to cross this continent to the desert of Arizona, or whether to stay here? What on earth could there be in this Word..."

I prayed; and when I opened the pages, my eyes fell on Hebrews chapter eleven verse nine. "By faith he sojourned in the land of promise, as in a strange country, dwelling in tabernacles with Isaac and Jacob, the heirs with him of the same promise." My eyes then went up a verse, and there it was: "By faith Abraham, when he was called to go out into a place which he should after receive for an inheritance, obeyed; and he went out, not knowing whither he went."

Although I usually don't base His leading in my life on only one verse of Scripture, I thought that if a man of faith such as Abraham could go from the safety of Ur of the Chaldees, and for a lifetime obediently follow after God, becoming a tent dweller and a pilgrim down here; then so could I! With that word I then traveled with the Daouds, first to Dallas, then on to Phoenix.

I had made a faith pledge for a certain number of months; and every time, just before the date it was due, I would receive twenty dollars which I could send back to Philadelphia.

This experience helped me step up to another rung on the ladder of faith. When I got up there, I found the Lord was not concerned with what you see or with what you have or don't have, but with what you will ***do*** when He speaks!

Wearing hats to church was a long established tradition in England. Here in Philadelphia, the Lord ***delivered*** me! When I was about eighteen and played the organ in church, I thought it was terrible when a young lady came into the service not wearing a hat. I believed I was doing the Lord a favor by wanting to give her one, that is, until I arrived in Philadelphia!

On New Year's Eve, I was attending a service at Fred Poole's church. Though I didn't realize it, this was a watch night service. After being served cake and coffee, it was announced that instead of going into the sanctuary, we were going to the chapel below.

The chapel held around four hundred people, and quickly began to fill up as I waited. Just before the clock struck – about one minute to midnight entering 1957– Pastor Poole stood and said, "Somebody has a word for 1957!"

Suddenly, without any warning from the Lord, the anointing dropped on me and covered me like a mantle. It was one of those exploding prophecies you simply had to give. This was one time I knew I ***must*** speak, and in the process the Lord wanted to teach me something. The word was just exploding in me. I slipped onto the floor and, putting my head down on the seat, prayed, "Lord, please take it away and give it to a man. I don't have a hat on!"

I always thought you had to be respectable, and that what you wore was so important. Although I knew the anointing, I still believed I must first have a hat on to be in order, and then the anointing would come. I had brought some hats with me to America, but didn't have one on that night. So, there I was with no hat!

The anointing didn't lift but instead increased; so I said, "Oh, God, help me." I just knew it was wrong, for the Bible said you should have something on your head, a covering. Such was the tradition in Scotland and England.

Suddenly, (the one and only time in my life the Lord spoke to me in this way) I heard His voice. I usually always heard Him on the inside, but this time I ***heard*** His voice; and He said, "The anointing is your covering. Why are you anxious?"

In that moment, I realized it was not a hat but the anointing that was my covering. I also realized it was more important for me to spend time before the Lord, getting my covering from Him before I went into a service, than getting my hat right. The hat was not important!

When the Lord said to me, "the anointing is your covering," I felt the shackles break and fall from my wrists and ankles. I then stood and gave the prophetic word for the coming year, declaring that "the lame would walk, the deaf would hear, and the blind would see." Brother Poole's church had experienced healings, but only occasionally at that time.

I then left Philadelphia and went to the desert of Arizona for three years. Later, I met someone there who said to me, "Do you remember that word you gave at the beginning of the year 1957 at midnight?" I said, "Yes, but I never heard anymore about it."

The person went on, "Well, nothing happened until October of that year when A. A. Allen came to the city of Philadelphia. People from all religious organizations filled the auditorium and the meetings were tremendous. Several cripples went from Fred Poole's church, along with some blind and deaf folk. The cripples returned from the meetings wheeling their wheel chairs; the deaf came back hearing; and the blind came back seeing. It didn't happen in Brother Poole's church, but it happened that year to that body!"

In Philadelphia, the Lord used my midnight experience to rid me of hats. Shortly thereafter, my thirty hats went sliding down in importance; and I never wore another hat. I left them all behind in Texas somewhere; I had no use for them after that!

Revival In A Cinema Amidst Mt. Sinai's Smoke

Chapter 8

In 1960, a few months after returning to England from the USA, David Greenow, a young evangelist who had been in Bible school with me, and I, rented an old cinema near Hereford, a town south of Stafford, which at the time had no Pentecostal witness.

That old cinema was so dirty inside it was impossible to clean! Apart from the Holy Ghost, the only fire we had was a solid fuel stove, which (when it felt like it) belched out more smoke than what went up the chimney. This sometimes caused a smokey fog like on Mt. Sinai to drift around us while we were preaching. I often wore a black velvet skirt because we were always sitting in soot!

Wyndom, a young fellow who was saved in those meetings was a "coal merchant," who delivered coal with his father. He came into the meeting one night as I was preaching; and becoming conscious of him, I could feel the burden that was upon his soul. When the service was over, he just sat there staring as if he had been hit with a brick. I walked down to him, took him by the hand and led him to the altar. Kneeling there, he continued to stare straight ahead, then soon began to confess his sin. Although Wyndom received salvation that night, the conviction of the Holy Spirit remained mightily upon him.

Returning the next night, he still seemed to be in a daze. With the life he had led, he couldn't understand or believe that God would forgive him and lift that burden of sin; and for forty-eight hours he walked in that dazed state. Suddenly, on the third night, the joy of God hit him and he began dancing. He danced that night as hard for the Lord as he had danced for the old devil, and the whole cinema danced and rocked with him!

So great was the change in Wyndom that one woman for whom he delivered coal came to the cinema to see what had happened to him. She used to be terrified of Wyndom and would leave her house when he and his father came to make a delivery. One morning she was home when he walked in, his coat and face black with coal dust. She said to him, "Oh, I'm so glad they had a change of boys. I couldn't put up with that fellow anymore. He was so terrible with all that cursing and swearing. What did they do with him?"

Turning to her, he said, "Oh, missus, I'm him. I went to that old cinema down the road, and God saved me and I don't swear and curse anymore." She said, "Where is it? I'll go there and see. What God can do for you, maybe He can do for my son!"

As God worked upon Wyndom's life, the joy of the Lord came, and he went all-out for God. When we held our water baptism, his mother, happy with the change in her son but afraid he would return to his old ways of stealing and drinking, was determined to go into the water with him.

She said to me, "Barbara, I'm so crippled with rheumatism that I fear water, and it's cold water at that. But I'm going into that river with my son."

With his old pals laughing on the bank, Wyndom and his mother both waded into the water. That frail little woman walked in behind her son, ready herself to go under in baptism. When they lifted her up out of the water, her arms shot up straighter than ever. In that cold water, every bit of rheumatism left her body; and she danced her way out of the river – healed!

Mary, a seventeen year old girl from a mental asylum, was brought by her mother to our meetings in the cinema. One night while we were singing, Mary started running up and down the aisle screaming, "I'm healed. I'm healed. I'm healed." Her mother, afraid she was going to become violent, and not understanding that Mary was trying to tell us that she was healed, ran after her, caught her and took her home. She put her daughter to bed that night (without the usual tranquilizers) and Mary slept like a baby, awaking normal the next morning. They returned the following night to the cinema to tell us. The change in Mary was marvellous, and her healing and deliverance became a great testimony for the Lord in that town.

One night in the service after Mary was wonderfully saved and delivered, she was sitting near the aisle by the old stove. As the evangelist was praying, I saw Mary suddenly stand up, the seat flipping up behind her. She stood back, looked up, and soon came running up to me. Throwing her arms around me, she said, "Oh, Sister Barbara, I've seen Jesus. Jesus is here!" As I looked at her, I knew she was quite sane. Taking her aside, I said, "Where is He? What happened?" Shaking with excitement she began telling me. Then I said to her, "No, wait, let's tell everybody," and I put the microphone in her hand.

She said, "I was sitting by the old stove that smokes, ready to bow my head for prayer, when a shadow fell across me. I thought somebody was standing there and wanted to come in; so I stood up, but nobody passed. When I looked up, I saw Jesus standing there."

"Describe Him, Mary," I said. She had been in an asylum since she was fifteen and didn't know anything about the Bible, but she began to describe Jesus from out of the Book of Revelation.

"Well," she said, "He had long hair and a long robe with something gold tied around His waist, and His toes were sticking out of His shoes. His garment was white. No, not white," she said, "Have you ever looked at water when the sun is shining on it and it's white, but it's not white; it's like a bright light? Or, it's like snow on the mountains when the sun shines on them, so white you can hardly look at it – more like a glaring bright light. That was the color He was wearing."

"Well, what happened, Mary?" I asked. She continued, "I looked at Him and He looked at me, not at anyone else, just at me. Then He smiled, and I saw all of heaven in His smile. Everything I ever needed of joy, peace, forgiveness – everything – was in His smile. And I suddenly felt I had everything in the world I would ever need for all of my life. Then he backed away, came up and stood by you and was gone."

Through Mary's vision of Jesus a number of folks were saved that night . They knew there was no way Mary could have known all of those things. The Bible says that it is not to the strong, but to the weak God gives the race. Hallelujah!

I should mention here that my father was always speaking on the second coming. Whether he began preaching from the Old Testament on Abraham, Moses,

Elijah or the prophets, or from the New Testament (the Acts of the Apostles was one of his favorites) – no matter where he started – he always ended up on the second coming. Every time! He was called, "the man of the eleventh hour." We always believed that the eleventh hour was the last hour, and that when we were speaking about the eleventh hour, we were speaking about the end. I remember thinking, "All I need to know now is the date!"

One night Mary came up to me before the service and said, "Do I look crazy?" I replied, "No, you look ordinary to me." She said, "I don't know, I think I'm going back to ***that*** way. I think I'm seeing things."

I asked her what she was seeing, and she answered, "Oh, it's not here; but when I was working in the laundry and pushing baskets, I kept seeing clocks everywhere! On the walls and wherever I looked, there would be clocks. I think I must be going nuts. I couldn't do anything for seeing clocks!"

Then I asked, "Mary, now tell me, was there anything similar about what you saw? What did the clocks say when you looked at them?" "Oh," she replied, "they all said the same thing. The little hand was close to twelve and the big hand would sweep around and stop at two minutes to twelve every time."

I said, "Mary, that revelation is not for you; it's for me. For I am the daughter of the man of the eleventh hour, but it's no longer the eleventh hour. It's two minutes to twelve." Through Mary's vision, God was showing me how much nearer we are to the time of the end and the second coming of our Lord. And, also, how near we are to the fulfilling of His promise to the prophet Joel that: "In the last days, saith God, I will pour out my Spirit upon all flesh! Your sons and your daughters shall prophesy, your young men shall see visions, and your old men shall dream dreams. And on my servants and on my handmaidens I will pour out in those days of my Spirit; and they shall prophesy."

Tent Revival
On The Sawdust Trail

Chapter 9

After the meetings in the cinema in 1960, I was called (by Pastor Shaw and evangelist Alan Ball) to help with a tent revival in Wolverhampton, a town just 18 miles from Stafford. The Lord gave us a tremendous revival. Under the Presence of God that old tent shook, as God poured out His Spirit. In three weeks of meetings, hundreds of healings took place.

The following is a letter I received some years after the tent revival from a lady who was miraculously healed:

> "Dear Sister Barbara,
>
> Ten years ago I was a terrible sufferer with discharging ulcers on both legs. The doctor at Royal Hospital, Wolverhampton gave up on me and said there was no cure, and that in less than two years my legs would be amputated. A few weeks after his diagnosis I was told by my dear mother that there was a faith healing campaign in Wolverhampton. I went and was met at the entrance by Allen Ball. The minute I came in I felt the power of God come over me. I did not know what it was until I stepped to the front for healing. When you put your hands upon me, I was instantly healed. I

came every night for more. You can never have too much of a good thing!

Mr. and Mrs. Shaw, Allen Ball, and you and your sister were the ones praying, and praise God! I still have my legs!"

In the tent meetings, we saw people with asthma instantly healed and skin conditions vanish. One man who came down the sawdust trail to be prayed for had a weeping eczema on his hands. He was an engineer but couldn't work because the oil used in his workplace made his skin break out. His fingers were all individually bandaged; and after being prayed for, he couldn't wait to remove the bandages and began ripping them off all the way back to his seat.

Moments later, in excitement, he came flying back up the aisle. With no fear or shyness, he thrust his hands out, waving them in my face. I thought, "My, have some manners!" My eyes were closed as I was praying for people, and I said to him, "Take your hands away." He replied, "Well, open your eyes!"

I opened my eyes and looked, and the skin on his hands was like the skin of a baby, white and pure. I began to cry realizing that while I was busy praying for that line of people, Jesus was standing so close to us in His love, healing and working miracles. Not only did the man receive healing, but he also gave his heart to the Lord that night.

Another man who came into the tent meetings was a leader in the Christian Brethren Church and a schoolmaster by profession. Since his denomination did not believe in the baptism in the Holy Spirit, he had been coming each night for a week just to observe. Then, after school each day, he would go home to his bedroom and pray; and God would speak a word into his heart.

In the services when my sister and I would get up to sing, I would always say a few words leading into the song. Every night for seven nights God gave this man a sign by leading me to say exactly what the Lord had spoken to him in his bedroom.

On the seventh night, he was convinced God was in that place and thought, "This is God! I must believe!" As the invitation was given, he came and stood before me asking prayer for healing. When I was about to put my hand on him, I said, "Brother, you're not here for healing, you're seeking the power of God in your life." Startled, he asked, "Who told you?" I replied that the Lord had spoken it to my heart. And he answered, "Yes, I am."

As we prayed for him, he received his first touch of spiritual power, just enough to give him an appetite. The next night he was back, well dressed as usual—English style, with his raincoat and umbrella over his arm. I was preaching on the baptism in the Holy Spirit; and at the end of the service, the altar was filled with mostly young people seeking that anointing from God.

While we were praying, I suddenly felt a drawing to go over to one side of the tent where a very tall, large man was standing. The Spirit impressed upon me that he was blocking something and that I should move him out of the way. As I led him to the side, standing right there behind him was this man seeking the baptism.

When I saw him I said, "Brother, come here; this is your night!" Before he could stop himself he said, "Sister, I can't understand it. Just this minute I was praying that if you would get this man out of the way, I would receive the Holy Spirit." While he was still speaking this in his heart to the Lord, I was pulling that fellow out of the way, and God was answering his prayer. Just as that happened, his sign was met and he believed God!

Standing there hungry and empty, forgetting all about his fancy suit and forgetting he was a leader in a church that didn't believe in the baptism he said, "I want this Holy Ghost!" As I put my hands on him to receive the Holy Spirit, my eyes were closed and I felt my hands going down. In his moment of faith the Holy Ghost fell on him and down he went into the sawdust!

Looking at him lying there, my first thought was, "Oh, he'll be a mess!"; and then I went on praying for the people. The next time I looked he was getting up from the ground, and was he a sight! Sawdust was in his hair, down his shirt and clinging to him everywhere. We brushed him off best we could, but he wasn't a bit bothered. He said, "Don't worry, I feel like a million dollars!"

Tent Meetings in Wolverhampton, England with Barbara Massie, Alan Ball, Pastor Fred Shaw and Anne Massie.

Northern Ireland: Sadie Shaw, Rosa Johnston, Barbara, Rita Woodrow & Joyce Johnston at Bethel Temple, Portglenone.

In Ireland 1959

Prophecy: The Hidden Spring of God

Chapter 10

Feeling completely worn out from the tent meetings in Wolverhampton, Anne and I traveled to Northern Ireland for a six-day rest. There we visited an Apostolic church where the men all knew my father. After the morning meeting, the elders of the church came to me and asked if I would speak that night. I said, "We are here for a break!" "Well," they replied, "We knew your father, and he preached here. Why won't you?"

Just coming from revival, the old choruses they sang in their morning service seemed especially dead, and I said to Anne under my breath, "It is like Ezekiel's boneyard in here!" Very unwillingly, I agreed to speak that night.

Ministering that evening under the spirit of revival still upon me from the tent meetings, that dead church arose and came to life! Later, I went to speak at another church and they, too, came alive. What had begun for me as a six-day rest ended up in a six-month stay!

It was during those six months of meetings in Ireland that my ministry first began to be revealed, and it came forth like a hidden spring of God. In those meetings, the first ones I ever held on my own, I began to come into a knowledge of what God had placed within me by the laying on of hands. Until then, I didn't really know the ministry God had for me; and very unexpectedly, I was finding it out.

I remember one service in particular where God suddenly broke in and the whole place was turned upside down. When I finished speaking, the people lined up for prayer — some for healing and others for different needs. As I went down the line praying for people, I found the Spirit of God was giving me personal revelation concerning their lives. One woman came up to me after the meeting and said, "Who told you my husband was dead?" I didn't even know she had a husband, but it must have come out as I prayed. Someone else said to me, "Who told you...?"

It was in those meetings I first began to realize there was something different happening in my ministry. As I was praying for people, the Lord was giving me words of knowledge for their lives. And, while I thought I was simply praying, I was actually prophesying and didn't know it. One of my colleagues from the Apostolic Bible school asked me, "What can you do with a ministry like this? Nobody does this. It's peculiar. How can you use this?" My reply was, "I don't know!" Somehow, though, in my mind I connected it with an experience Anne and I had on the streets of London some years before.

On that particular occasion in London, Anne and I were out shopping in a market place that had little booths filled with different kinds of produce and goods for sale. We noticed a crowd of people standing together in the middle of the area, and I said to Anne, "Let's go see what's cooking over there." Peering through the crowd, we saw an ordinary looking little woman standing with her purse over her arm and a shopping bag at her feet. Apparently she had been out shopping and had stopped to tell people their fortunes for money. She had a spirit of divination and was revealing various things about their lives that nobody knew.

We listened as she spoke to an older white-haired man concerning his wife who had died. Supposedly his wife was giving him a message through this medium, telling him she was happy and busy getting things fixed up on the other side, and that he should continue with his shopping. Thinking the medium had actually contacted his wife, this poor man was standing there in the middle of London with tears running down his cheeks, weeping.

The Spirit of God got hold of me and I felt a holy anger – the kind of anger I feel when the enemy rises up. I thought, "The rottenness of the enemy coming up here on the streets to deceive the people." Knowing that greater was He that was in us than he that was in her, I said to Anne, "We're going to break this thing. You go over on that side and I'll stay here on this side; and when I make a motion, begin to pray." I stepped behind a large man standing near me, and Anne got behind someone else on the other side of the crowd. We began to plead the blood of Christ and to bind the spirit in that medium.

As we were binding that spirit of divination, a lady came up to her who was obviously pregnant. The medium asked the lady to cross her hand with silver, and then she began to think of what to say. Opening her eyes and looking around, she said to the lady, "Well, you're going to have a baby." To which the lady replied, "I know that." The medium, glancing my way and then Anne's way said, "Ah, you'll be having a bit of sickness in the morning." And the lady replied, "I know that; I've had that." Then she said some other silly thing that everybody knew. The poor medium was getting all mixed up and couldn't get through to her spirit teacher; we were cutting her off. She would turn around, look both ways to see who was doing this to her, but she couldn't tell. Anne and I were hidden from sight as we were pleading the blood of Christ, and the medium couldn't receive anything for this lady.

Next, a man came and stood in front of her. She raised her eyes to heaven and then dropped them to the ground. She looked left and right, but she was blank. She couldn't get one thing because the blood of Christ was covering that group. All of a sudden she did a quick glance left and right, put her money in her purse, grabbed her shopping bag and dashed through the crowd. I could see her little legs running down the road and I thought, "There goes the old devil on the run!"

As I stood on that London street, still a young nurse, I said in my heart to the Lord, "If that woman can give her life to the enemy and use a familiar spirit to deceive and rob people…if she can do that for the devil, Lord, why can't you make me your spiritual medium for people who need help?"

I had never seen or heard of anyone being a spiritual medium for the Lord; but I believe the Lord allowed that experience to come my way to inspire me to ask. God will give us the very thing that we ask for; and the Lord took me at my word. Now, not so many years later, the Lord was bringing me into what was then an unknown ministry.

For the first time, here in Ireland, the Lord began to move through me prophetically with a personal word of knowledge and of wisdom, revealing the secrets of men's hearts, and bringing understanding and direction to the workings of God in people's lives. I heard one

Irish woman who was standing in the prayer line say, "Begorra, that girl just told me all my life story! There's something strange going on in this place!" I realized, too, that some were becoming alarmed, wondering if I would reveal something they did not want known. But the Lord does not expose people. He forgives and covers sin when we confess to Him.

During this time, as my ministry was coming forth, the devil rose up in a storm against me; and I began to suffer persecution. Never having seen this kind of ministry before, some said I was a witch. Others said I was a spiritualist medium. One preacher was going around warning people not to listen to me saying I was using mental telepathy. Nobody understood what was happening through me; they had never experienced personal prophecy or seen a prophetic ministry operate like this.

One night after a meeting, I heard the whole band of preachers talking against me, saying things about me that I couldn't imagine they could have even possibly thought. So much was being said against me at that time, that I wondered what else they could say!

I had gone to Ireland as a respectable nurse, but, through all the opposition I was experiencing, I had now lost my reputation. I lost my pride and everything you can lose; I became as nothing. Before that, I thought I was something! In Stafford, I was a nursing sister partly in charge of a hospital. The police, the ambulance men, everybody in the city knew me and respected me. But now, here in Ireland, I lost all of that. I was nobody, and I felt like dirt! I was, however, finding myself caught up into something in God that was greater than me. In my affliction, I bowed before the Lord; down and down I went until the mill of God ground me into powder.

This was the time when the prophetic gift was beginning to flow, springing up like a fountain from deep within me. One of the first meetings where this happened was particularly memorable. After preaching the message, I always made time to pray for the people. This one night, as people were passing under my hands for prayer, the Spirit of God was speaking through me to each one in a personal word of revelation. After praying for a length of time, I came to the point where I had closed my eyes and someone was holding my arms up and directing me where to put my hands. With my eyes closed and not knowing whether it was a man or woman upon whom my hands were laid, I continued in what I thought was praying (which was actually prophesying), until the whole church had passed before me one by one. I became so caught up in the Spirit that I was having difficulty staying on my feet. The Irish folk, thinking I was fainting, were holding me up, and then put a chair under me for support. Someone even ran out to a café near the church and brought me a cup of tea. They had never seen anything like this before; it was all so new, they didn't know what to do; and I didn't understand it myself.

In that same service, as I was speaking, an Irish girl sitting in the front row saw the Lord standing on my left side holding a scroll. He was beckoning for her to come up and read it. She had seen Him standing there the previous night as well. When she told me about it that second night, I said to her, "If it happens tomorrow, obey the Lord and come up, because I know what is on that scroll."

The next night in the meeting, sensing the Lord's presence beside me, I looked down at her and she started to come up toward the platform. Standing beside me she opened her Bible to Isaiah 61.

"The Spirit of the Lord God is upon me; because the Lord hath anointed me to preach good tidings unto the meek; he hath sent me to bind up the brokenhearted, to proclaim liberty to the captives, and the opening of the prison to them that are bound; to proclaim the acceptable year of the Lord, and the day of vengeance of our God; to comfort all that mourn; to appoint unto them that mourn in Zion, to give unto them beauty for ashes, the oil of joy for mourning, the garment of praise for the spirit of heaviness; that they might be called trees of righteousness, the planting of the Lord, that he might be glorified."

As she was reading that portion from Isaiah, I knew at that moment I was receiving my commission from the Lord. God was giving me His special endorsement, confirming my calling and imparting to me His authority and anointing to fulfill that calling.

However, I barely had time to enjoy the tremendous thrill of having the Lord stand at my side commissioning me, when the devil appeared to me at midnight in the form of darkness. As I was sitting in the corner of my room, exhausted from the long meetings, and holding onto the radiator trying to keep warm, the devil appeared and spoke audibly to me saying, "Before morning, I will smash you! I will destroy you, and I will destroy your ministry." And with that a cloud of darkness fell all round me. It was a terrible hit! It came all in the same night — the awesomeness of the Lord coming in His wonderful presence commissioning me, and then the devil hard on His heels!

Alone in my room in that midnight hour, my mind flooded with all the terrible accusations and negative things people were saying against me. I thought, "There *must* be something wrong with me. I must have missed God somewhere, or I must have grieved the Holy Spirit." Thinking and wondering "what have I done wrong," I found myself in a place of deep darkness and despair. For about forty-eight hours I just walked around my room, fasting and praying in agony before God. Unaware of whether it was day or night, light or dark, I searched my heart to find out what I could have done that would have brought all this suffering upon me.

In agony before God I cried, "Where did I fail? Did I give them cause? What did I do?" Walking the floor weeping, I said, "God, I can't take this. I can't take it!" Then the Lord drew near and began to show me in II Corinthians 12:7 what the thorn in the flesh and the buffeting was that Paul had suffered.

> *"And lest I should be exalted above measure through the abundance of the revelations, there was given to me a thorn in the flesh, the messenger of Satan to buffet me, lest I should be exalted above measure."*

God revealed to me that the thorn in the flesh can be a person, a messenger of Satan, usually somebody on your own level who will come in and buffet you, hitting you where you will be affected most. Because of the revelation of the Spirit that is coming, the thorn also comes to keep humble the one who is carrying the truth. There has to be that buffeting and striking down, lest at any time the one who is called of God would raise himself up, and then be destroyed because of the weight of the revelation upon him. There have been many great leaders who have gone down because their heads swelled with pride.

What is a thorn? When you have a thorn, you are aware of it; you feel it, but you can't get at it. You say, "I've got a thorn here; I can't see it, but oh, it's giving me trouble." And when people start to talk about you, and men persecute you, the first thing you want to do is to defend yourself. However, just try and put your finger on it; you never can. Illusively, it is always, "someone said." But when they are asked, their answer is, "*they* never said; *they* only just *heard*." And you'll never find that thorn, for God has allowed it to come in to keep you low.

The Spirit of God spoke to me and said, "You can go around the world preaching the gospel, but if you will not receive the thorn, you will not have the revelation. If you take the thorn, then you will have the revelation. If you will fulfill your calling, if you will fulfill the purpose for which I brought you forth from the womb, then you must embrace the buffeting. For I will give you revelation upon revelation – and you will be buffeted – but I will love you and my hand will be upon you."

Kneeling there in the darkness, wondering what to do, I thought, "I can just be an ordinary preacher and escape the lash, escape the tongue and escape the thorn. Or, I can receive it and go on with what God is giving me." The Lord said to me, "What will you do?"

Considering the short time we have in this life, I realized that if we can be a hundredfold for God, we can have a hundredfold back from Him. I pondered: " If I don't fulfill the calling on my life, or if I fail God in the hour when He is asking for men and women who will endure the thorn, then...?" So in the darkness of that room, in the darkness of my heart, I made my choice.

The Lord also gave me the scripture from Isaiah 42:18,19:

> *"Hear, ye deaf; and look, ye blind, that ye may see. Who is blind, but my servant? Or deaf, as my messenger that I sent? Who is blind as he that is perfect, and blind as the Lord's servant?"*

"None is so blind and none is so deaf…" Reading that I thought, "Isn't that awful! Nobody is as deaf? What kind of servant is this? One who can't see or hear anything?" Then, in amazement, I read the next part: "And none so perfect." I thought, "What does this mean?"

The Lord then revealed to me that when He gives someone the key to unlock prisons and bring forth those who are bound, or to bring those who sit in darkness into the light, then this servant of the Lord must be blind to his enemies. He must be deaf to what they say, yet also perfect before God. In the midst of the persecution, the Lord made me to know my problem was that I was seeing and hearing my enemies, feeling their taunts and was all too aware of what was going on!

God's purpose through all of my suffering and affliction was to lift me into a higher realm. The devil was using flesh and blood to come against me. In reality, however, it was not flesh and blood; it was not people who were fighting me; it was principalities and powers in heavenly places that wanted to bring me down and keep me from rising into the higher places God purposed to take me.

Throughout my six months in Ireland, I had revivals going on in two cities. Because of the force of the opposition against me, someone said to me, "Go back to England!" And I said, "I will not! I will not go back to England!!!" The Lord had spoken directly to me and said, "When they persecute you in one town, flee to the next." I returned then to the other city and continued with the revival there, and it really took off. However, persecution soon followed, coming from the other city; and I knew it would come.

I was seeking God during this time with prayer and fasting for the meetings, and I became very thin. One night I came to the service with my eyes swollen and red from crying. I had been weeping and weeping, wiping my eyes with cold water trying to make them look normal. As I played the piano and led the singing, I was asking the Lord for a message. Feeling a great pressure upon me, and being so concerned with what was happening, I hadn't been able to think about what I was going to speak on that night.

While at the piano the scripture came to me, "Rejoice, and be exceeding glad." "Well," I thought, "that's something! My eyes are red from tears, my heart is broken, and the people are downcast because they are all feeling sorry for me. I can't speak on that!"

The Lord said, "'Rejoice, and be exceeding glad: for great is your reward in heaven…' Speak on it!" I said to Him, "I can't; I feel like crying." The Lord said again, "Speak on it!" I tried to think of what I had spoken on previously that I could preach again – but, you cannot say "NO" to the Lord! I had to obey God!

I knew that no other message could be preached that night except for what the Lord had given me. There at the piano I made an arrangement with the Lord – I do that only in emergencies, when I am out on a limb and just hanging there! I said, "All right, Lord, I will go up and speak on 'rejoice, and be exceeding glad,' and I will try to be glad. But, You must put the 'exceeding' in, because I cannot be exceeding glad!"

As I left the piano and went up before the people, my face was long and my eyes were red from crying. I began reading the text in Matthew 5, and came to the part in verse 11 which says, "Blessed are ye, when men shall revile you, and persecute you, and shall say all manner of evil against you falsely, for my sake." Not able to even smile, I went on reading: "Rejoice, and be exceeding glad: for great is your reward in heaven..."

Shortly into preaching the message, my face began brightening into a smile; and somewhere down the line, speaking became easier and easier. Instead of laboring under the burden that was upon my heart, I found that, after a while, I had no burden and my heart wasn't aching anymore. As I went on, I didn't have to try and be glad, for I was beginning to get happy, and my spirit was becoming lighter.

As I looked out upon the congregation, I could see the people were reflecting me. They were relaxed, and gradually, bit by bit, beginning to smile and become happy, too. The happier I got; the happier they got. The Holy Spirit was moving in that place, and I was experiencing a happiness that was way beyond myself. I felt myself being caught up in the Spirit; and I said within, "Lord, You're doing it! You're putting the 'exceeding' in." I was being pushed out of my own measure and into a measure in God I had never been in before – and it is when you are out of yourself and in God, that revival rolls.

After a while, I became "exceeding glad," and could not speak for laughing. As I laughed, the people laughed, until we were all laughing in the Spirit while I was preaching this word. Suddenly, I began to see those big Irish giants who had spoken against me dwarf, until they became just little men. All those devils of fear and doubt and unbelief that had pressed upon me vanished, and both me and the people were being delivered.

When I was finished speaking, a man of about sixty walked up from the back and stood before me. His face was very pale and tense. He said, "I want prayer," and then publicly began to confess: "Seven years ago this church was visited by God and I was in the move, but something happened and I lost my blessing. I have been a terrible husband and father. I need deliverance; I can't live like this anymore." He had allowed an evil spirit to come into his life because he had spoken against different ones and different situations. He was a lonely man, living in darkness, and tormented by evil spirits. He had become cruel to his wife and children and would not let them come to church.

By this time in the meeting, I was way out of my "measure" and into the blessing of God. Immediately I replied, "Brother, the Lord can change you in a moment." I began to rebuke those evil spirits, and they came flying out, naming themselves as they left. There was no effort at all; as soon as he confessed, they had to come out. In the power of God, he was instantly delivered.

Turning around looking at the folks he said, "You know, I feel clean all over, like I have just been swept clean inside." We then put our hands on him and commanded that he receive the Holy Spirit, and that those areas in his life now be filled with the presence of God. Just as we touched him, he threw up his hands and began to praise the Lord in other tongues. For seven years he had been under this terrible cloud. Now his white, pale face was suddenly flushed with the joy of the Lord as he began to worship God.

Sitting on the edge of the platform behind me, he began to laugh. It was the strangest laugh I had ever heard; he hee-hawed like a donkey. We were laughing before but when this man began hee-hawing, we all went weak with laughter. We laughed until we could laugh no more. At midnight he was still laughing. This was the "exceeding glad" — an "exceeding without measure!"

As we were leaving the service between midnight and one in the morning, we looked out the door and here he was, his name was Jimmy, trying to get on his bicycle to go home. He would put one leg over the bicycle and then fall off the other side. After half a dozen tries, I said to him, "Jimmy, you'll never get home that way. In the state you're in, you better push your bicycle and walk." He answered, "I suppose you're right;" and off he went.

Since I was the only one with a car (the others had horses and carts and bicycles), several rode with me to go home. While driving up the main street of this small quiet village, past a big Catholic monastery and it's huge graveyard, we had the windows open, and in the warm night air we began to hear something. It was a hee-haw, hee-haw, hee-haw. Stopping in front of the two big pillars at the entrance of the graveyard, I said to the others, "Surely, he's not in there!" We called out, but the only answer we got was, "hee-haw, hee-haw." As we sat and waited, eventually Jimmy came pushing his bicycle out of the darkness, from between the two pillars and through the big gate.

As he staggered through the two entry pillars, I said to him, "Jimmy, how did you get in there?" He said, "I made a wrong turn; and when I realized I was in the graveyard, I just sat down on a tombstone and began to laugh in the joy of the Lord!"

I realized then just how truly the Lord had delivered him from the terrors of darkness. Before the Lord touched him that night, Jimmy was scared of everything; but now there was not a bit of fear in him – even in a graveyard in the middle of the night!

Because I was willing to take the burden and let the Spirit of God break through, a spring was opened in Jimmy's life. His home was changed, the devils were cast out, and his wife and children could live in peace – all because God put the "exceeding" in. Of ourselves we can do nothing, but the Lord can put an "exceeding" into our lives that will bring us out on top every time.

Those folks never forgot that night, and it was spoken of over and over many times. But none of them ever knew what had taken place between the Lord and me, and *how* the Lord put that well of "exceeding" in my life. I, too, never forgot that night; and I have never gone back into that place of despondency.

The forces of the enemy, recognizing the prophetic mantle and prophetic ministry that God was bringing me into in that hour, had risen up against me. Through the fires of persecution I was reduced to ashes; but out of the ashes of that experience, I rose into a different realm in God altogether. The Lord brought me through that storm; and when He did, all that talk against me just became like air to me. And I realized then that if I were to move in a higher dimension in God, I was going to have opposition.

The Lord will do a marvellous job of defending us if we don't try to do it ourselves. As God was moving and pouring out His Spirit where I was ministering, the people from the first church came over and publicly confessed that they had spoken against me falsely and against what the Lord was doing. Though it took some weeks of brokenness and waiting, it finally all got sorted out. But it happened because I stood my ground in the midst of persecution.

We will not find anywhere in scripture where God serves His gifts and ministries on a platter. The Word speaks of His treasures found in darkness. It is out of the darkness of searching, out of the darkness of our experience, and in the twilight of suffering, that we find great treasure: gold, pearls, nuggets and gems, gifts and ministries – treasures of great value which come out of our experience in God, because we are willing to pay the price.

At 50 Stone Road, Stafford, England:
Barbara and Anne, with parents Margaret and W. W. Massie

At Hockley Pentecostal Church: Barbara, William W., Anne

New Wine — You Will Smile Again

Chapter 11

From my early days, I sought the Lord and desired to be used of Him, but I never considered the prophetic ministry. In fact, I didn't particularly want to prophesy because I always thought that prophets and apostles were "way up there," and I was just a nurse. That was it, and never the twain shall meet! Nor had I ever considered the ministry of new wine, when in 1962, the Lord told me I would be a bearer of new wine and fresh oil. These things all just happened! And with them came the suffering. There is a price to pay for following the Lord, even though at times we may not be aware we are paying it. Such was the case when Anne and I went to Ireland for a six-day rest in late 1960 and I ended up staying for six months of ministry — the last six months of my mother's life.

Shortly after returning from Ireland, I was preaching a weekend convention at Hockley Pentecostal Church in Birmingham. It was there on Easter Sunday morning, the news came to Anne and me — the Lord had taken my mother home to glory in her sleep. Anne and I had dealt with thousands of patients and attended to hundreds of deaths, but when the Lord came for my mother, I was away from home preaching. It was dreadful!

My mother was a very godly and precious woman, and her death felt like the end of everything for me in 1961. I had given up years of my life in ministry away from home and had seen the Lord heal so many others in healing lines. Deep in my heart I wondered why He didn't heal my mother. I was very broken-hearted, and even a little bitter toward the Lord.

Six months after burying my mother, my father also went home to be with the Lord. During the six months between their deaths, Miss Fisher and Miss Reeves, pioneer pastors of Hockley Pentecostal Church, invited me to speak every weekend. At this time I was in a very low state of health. Before returning home from America in 1959, I had neglected my health through prayer and fasting in the desert of Arizona (then later in Ireland). Not that fasting is bad; it is good for you, but you have to use wisdom; and this I learned the hard way. My health was broken and so was my heart, and I truly thought I would never smile again.

During one of the weekend meetings in Hockley, a prophecy was given to the congregation through a girl from Scotland. The word began, "Oh, you've said in your heart, you'll never smile again. You've said this and that..." – things I had said, not to anybody, but just to myself. I was the preacher that morning and I was sure everyone would know it was me to whom the Lord was speaking! The prophetic word went on: "But you're going to start climbing now, and every step will be uphill until you hit the mountain top. Then you'll smile, and you'll never stop smiling."

That word was so real to me at that time. After my mother's death I just had lost heart; and it didn't seem like I would ever smile again, but I knew the Lord was speaking to me that day! The fulfillment of that word didn't come in a day or a week, but the time did come when all that sorrow was behind me. Suddenly, I could smile and laugh again, because "joy had come in the morning." The Lord allows nighttime, but when light breaks in the eastern sky, it is always the sign of the dawning of a new day — not a day of sadness but of joy!

In 1962, I was on my way to Holland, a land still mourning the effects of the German occupation during the war. A lady and her son drove me down to Devon and Cornwall on the south coast of England, where I was to have a meeting before crossing the English channel. Sick in body and broken-hearted, I wasn't feeling like much of a missionary, but the Lord had said, "Go!"

Arriving at a beautifully thatched roof farmhouse with a church building behind it, we went straight into the meeting. After the songs and testimonies, I waited for them to introduce me and call me up to speak. But nothing happened. I remember thinking that after coming all that way, I was not going to have enough time to preach. In fact, nobody seemed to take any notice of me; so I sat and waited.

I noticed a big man at the back (an Englishman who had been a missionary in Brazil) thumbing through his Bible when, suddenly, he marched up and started to preach. After preaching hard, he walked down the aisle, and standing by me said, "Hi girl, you should have preached this morning. I waited and waited."

"So did I!" I replied. I was waiting for the call; he was waiting for me to move.

He asked, "Did you not know to go up there?"

"Yes, when I was asked."

"You won't be asked here; we're different down here."

"You sure are!" I replied.

I had never been with people who were so open to the Spirit that when they came together they didn't announce the speaker. The one who was speaking was just supposed to go up without being introduced! God at times uses odd things to do something within you. If I had preached and all had gone well, I would have been off to Holland, but I wasn't ready for Holland. Holland was a weeping country; and I, too, was still weeping from the loss of my mother!

However, I was quite stirred up thinking I had missed God in the meeting. I felt the Lord had sent me there with a message for the people and I was determined to preach it, though I wondered how it could be, as there were no more services until later in the week.

The next day, Monday, I began fasting. There is power in the dual weapons of fasting and prayer, to open doors that are otherwise shut and bring to pass things in your life you never thought possible.

"I won't be eating today, thank you!" I said to the lady at the farmhouse, as she put the biggest roast you ever saw into the oven.

"Nobody comes into this farmhouse kitchen and doesn't eat," she said. "I thought you were leaving for Holland?"

I answered, "No! No, I'm not going to Holland *yet*!"

If the Lord had not touched my pride on Sunday in front of everybody, I would have been on my way to Holland. But I changed my ticket! I was beginning to have the feeling God was in this somehow; I sensed there was something unborn within me that had to come forth in that place before I could leave. Holland needed me, but they didn't need me the way I was.

That night, those of us who were staying at the farmhouse were sitting in the kitchen. I was near this big open fire, feeling quite geared up, though not knowing for what, when a knock came on the door. Soon there was another knock, then several more knocks, and different ones just drifted in until we had about forty people in that kitchen area.

Someone said, "Why don't we have church?" And someone else chimed, "That's just what we were thinking!" And I thought, "You don't know what's coming to you!"

Now, I had not eaten all day, but they had. Some were full of chicken and steak, but I was full of power – like pulling an elastic band back before letting go. If you pull that band way back, whatever you are shooting at is really going to get it! That is just what the Lord does with me sometimes – He pulls me back, holds me back, and then lets me go!

The big Englishman was there, and I was keeping my eye on him. When he said, "I think we should have church." I quickly said, "Let's all kneel and pray." I thought, "You're not getting the better of me this time!'

While down praying, I asked the Lord, "What am I going to preach? For I *am* going to preach!" Just that quick, the Lord gave me the thought of binding and loosing.

Ten minutes later we were still praying, and I was getting hot by this fire. It was then I saw the Englishman on his knees opening his Bible. I said to myself, "Not again, brother, not again!" Immediately, I stood up and said, "O.K. Everybody up! Turn in your Bibles to Matthew 18, verse 18."

"Verily I say unto you, Whatsoever ye shall bind on earth shall be bound in heaven: and whatsoever ye shall loose on earth shall be loosed in heaven."

It was the first time I had ever preached on this subject and I was on my toes, biting out every word. The Spirit of God was upon me, the fire of God within me, and the fire in the fireplace, blazing hot, behind me. Due to the shape of the room, I had to stand by the fireplace to get the people's eye, and I was cooking inside and out! I thought, "My Lord, I feel like roast turkey ready for serving!"

As I was speaking, the Holy Spirit was beginning to fall; and at the same time, I was becoming aware of something very unusual happening to me. I was experiencing a feeling of unsteadiness on my feet and a sensation that the ceiling and walls were moving in and out. I thought, "I wonder what's wrong with me? I didn't eat dinner, so it couldn't be food." My eyes were losing focus and everything was blurring; but I kept on preaching, not sure if I was looking straight at the people or not. When it came time to put my hands on people, I knew for sure something was wrong with me. Instead of one head I could see three, and I didn't know which head to put my hands on!

Glancing around, I saw the big Englishman looking very strangely, as though he were having trouble focusing on me. I thought, "Oh, there is something wrong with him!" Suddenly, WHAM! With a terrible thump, he fell off his chair.

A very properly dressed English businessman, umbrella in hand and raincoat over his arm, had come in earlier. Removing his hat, he sat down with an air of refinement. But now his hat was on the floor and he was barely staying in his seat. Then, WHAM! He, too, was on the floor. I looked around and no one was sitting straight anymore. They were all getting a bit lopsided. I was very aware that the Spirit of God was coming in a way that I had never seen before.

Over in the corner, a young man began barking like a dog. I had heard that before, both in my father's meetings and in A. A. Allen's meetings in Arizona. It didn't take any discernment to know that he was demon possessed. As I prayed for him, the Lord gave me revelation concerning his condition, and in no time, he was delivered.

Somewhat dazed, he asked, "What happened, and what was that barking?"

"That was you!" I answered.

"Barking, was I? I never did that in my life!"

When I asked if he had ever been in a meeting before, he replied, "What meeting?" He was on vacation from Birmingham and was walking up the street. Hearing the singing and thinking it was a tavern, he had come in and sat down.

"Aren't they all drunk on the floor?" he asked.

"No! Nobody's drinking here." Then, pondering what was happening, I said, "Well, I guess maybe we are drunk!"

"That's what I thought it was!" he replied.

This young man, not knowing the Lord, came into the farmhouse kitchen that night and was beautifully saved and delivered. After the devil was cast out of him, we put our hands on him and he began to praise God in another language and could no longer stay on his feet. By this time, people were lying everywhere, slain by the Holy Spirit and intoxicated in His presence.

Judging by what I saw in those around me and how I was feeling, I knew God was giving me an experience in the new wine. When those early believers, having received the Holy Spirit on the day of Pentecost, were accused of being full of new wine, Peter rose up and said,

> *"For these are not drunken AS YE SUPPOSE, seeing it is but the third hour of the day. But this is that which was spoken by the prophet Joel: And it shall come to pass in the last days, saith God, I will pour out of My Spirit upon all flesh..."*

Although I had seen God pour out His Spirit before, I had never known what it was to be intoxicated in the Spirit. This was an entirely new experience for me, different from the baptism of the Holy Spirit which I received when I was 14, and different from the new anointing I experienced in 1951 which totally changed my life. There in Devon I began to imbibe the new wine of the Spirit, and I was too hungry, too thirsty, and too needy to care about how it came. It seemed the less I cared about how I looked to those around me, the more God imparted to me. As the meetings continued through that week, I found drunkenness of the Spirit coming upon me every night, and upon the people as well. Also as this blessing of God increased, I found that while under the power of God, I was still able to control myself and continue ministering to the people.

In these farmhouse meetings, I realized God was pouring upon us the same new wine of His Spirit that Peter and the disciples experienced. Only one other time had anything like this ever happened. It was in 1960 (two years before) in Stafford, when a group of us had rented a hall and held meetings. At the close of the meetings after everyone had gone except the caretaker, about a dozen of us, (including the evangelists, my sister and I and a few others) decided to join hands and worship the Lord at the front of the hall. As we were standing in a circle, I began to feel my head getting light and as if I were losing control of my limbs. I thought, "If I don't hold on to somebody, I'm going to fall over!" I tried to shut my eyes, but that was worse.

To balance myself, I began leaning on the person next to me; as it happened, we were all doing the same thing. While standing together quietly praising the Lord, someone to my left gave way and fell. Since we were leaning on one another for support, when one fell, we all started to fall. Then all twelve of us went running sideways (like when you stumble over something and your feet run to catch up with your head)! I noticed we were headed toward the wall and I thought, "Oh, we won't fall; we'll just land against that wall."

What I didn't see was a door, painted the same color as the wall, with a FIRE sign above it. With a crash, we hit the bar across the fire-door. It swung wide open and we all went flying through and landed in a heap at the feet of the caretaker, who had been standing just outside the door. As we extricated ourselves from the pile, none of us could see or walk straight. Startled, the caretaker said, "I thought this was a religious meeting. If I'd known it were a bottle party, I would have come, too! I didn't know you were going to get drunk!"

DRUNK! We hadn't thought we were drunk! But when he looked at us and said that, I thought, "Are we all drunk? How did we get drunk? And how did we fly through that door and not break our necks?"

That experience in Stafford was just an introduction, a taste of what the Lord had for me. However, it was in the farmhouse in Devon where the Lord gave me a real *baptism* in the "new wine" – and that was my preparation for Holland!

—✧—

As God was pouring out His Spirit upon us in Devon, the Lord spoke to me and said, "I will make you a ***bearer*** of new wine and of fresh oil." I thought, "Well, that's joyful news, but I don't feel like bearing anything!" Besides, I had never heard of a ministry like that, and I wasn't sure what the Lord meant. He also said, "And you will go to those who sit and mourn in dark places."

When I finally arrived in Holland, I was met by Bella, my interpreter, who was originally from Scotland. She took me first to a large Assemblies of God convention, which should have been full of life; but their fastest songs were slower than our funeral hymns! There was no touch of the Spirit or of blessing; no one smiled and no one said "Amen." Everything seemed so slow and dead; I thought to myself, "Can these bones live?"

Noticing a number of pastors at this convention, Bella said to me, "Come, Sister Barbara; I'll introduce you, and God will open the way." I, on the other hand, had an awful feeling from previous experience that it would not be man who would open the door. Consequently, every preacher I was introduced to promptly closed the door in my face. Very politely they would say, "We'll be glad to see you in the service sometime!" (As in Ireland, the Dutch also were not accepting of women preachers.) All the pastors shook hands with me and said they hoped I had a nice holiday, but none of them wanted me. I thought, "Well, the Lord wants me. I'm not here on a ***holiday***!"

Earlier in the day, however, the Lord ***had*** opened a door for me, but I didn't want it. A little man, who had been born crippled and was confined to a wheelchair, had approached me and said, "Will you come and speak at our place?"

"Is it a church?" I asked.

"Well, it's not a church. It's the back of a store where we have our services." I thought, "I don't want to go inside the back of a store!"

"I'll talk to you later, brother," I replied. But in my heart, I meant a flat, "No!"

At the end of the service, as Bella and I were leaving, there waiting at the door was this little man in the wheelchair. Again he asked, "Are you coming?" By now all the preachers had passed me by, and I thought, "***This*** is the way." Humbled, I answered, "Yes, I will come!"

Sunday morning, Bella and I arrived at the jeweler's shop where the meeting was held. The door was open and we walked through, past the displays of beautiful Dutch jewelry, gorgeous rings and gold watches, to the lovely parlor behind the shop where several Dutch people were already gathered.

After preaching, I began calling people up for prayer. At one point, I lost my interpreter, as Bella went down under the power along with the person I was praying for! It was then I noticed a beautiful blonde girl of about thirty-four, standing in the doorway of the parlor dressed in her night attire with a housecoat around her. As I looked at her, the Lord showed me the devil afflicting her in the form of an insane spirit. Forgetting our language difference, I walked over to her and said, "You have an insane spirit; and you have been in and out of asylums all your life, but it's all over now. The devil is coming out, and God is going to heal you in the name of Jesus Christ." I prayed for her and she fell to the floor and was instantly delivered.

Still in her housecoat, she got up, ran into the parlor and fell on her father's neck, hugging him and telling him and everyone else how the Lord had delivered her and set her free. Though the Dutch rarely demonstrate their emotions, here was this father and daughter openly embracing and weeping together. And as they wept, everyone in the room wept with them. Her father, a Jewish man, was the owner of the jewelry shop. His daughter was very precious to him; and now the Lord had restored her.

When I came back that night for the meeting, the place was overflowing with people. I said to Bella, "News gets around!"

"Oh," she said, "You don't know what happened! It is a great thing the Lord has done for this man's daughter. Since she was seventeen years old, she has been given to depression and been in and out of asylums. Her deliverance is a marvellous miracle, and this afternoon her father picked up his phone and called all his friends and relatives and told them what God had done!"

The next night the meeting was held in a church, and when I arrived, the church was so packed I couldn't get in. I said to the man at the door, "You have to let me in; I am the preacher!"

The pastors of the Assemblies of God churches, from that area of Holland, were all in the meeting. Together they came to me and said, "There are seven of us, and we want you to come to each of our churches." God has His way of opening doors! As I went from church to church preaching, many of the people who were weary of bondage and weary of their needs being unmet began to follow me. Many of their faces soon became familiar to me as we moved from place to place. Then I noticed something remarkable happening – God was changing that sorrowful look upon their faces into brightness and the joy of the Lord!

One of the meetings where I was invited to speak in Holland was held in a large fancy house with a spacious living room. After preaching, I called forward those who wanted prayer. On one end of the prayer line was a happy-faced little woman; and on the other end stood a giant of a woman who was over six feet tall, had big hands, big muscles, wore big shoes, and dressed like a man. She was a "market gardener" who grew her own plants and vegetables to sell in her stand in the market place. The Lord said to me, "She's your first one. Call her." And the devil whispered, "Pray for her last. Pray for the sweet-faced little woman first. She will be easier." But the Lord said, "No, take the big woman."

To me this powerful looking woman seemed to be the hardest one in the whole place to start with. I didn't want to call her first, but I knew if the devil whispered to call her last, then I must call her first! Through my interpreter, I said to her, "You come, sister, God has something for you." She was from the high Dutch Episcopalian church and had no knowledge of the things of the Spirit. When she stepped toward me, she reached out and shook my hand!

"Do you know the Lord?" I asked her.

"Ya, ya, ya, ya!" she replied in Dutch.

As I began to pray for her, I was on my toes stretching to lay my hand on top of her head. Gradually, I noticed it was becoming easier to reach her, and when I looked, her knees were folding like a melodian. She was coming down! When she was about eye-level and her knees would not bend any more, she collapsed flat onto the floor causing quite a commotion. The people jumped back as the chairs went flying! No one expected *her* to go down! Although folk were supposed to have their eyes shut, they were all watching and laughing; and I knew by their faces she was the last one they thought would be open to the Spirit's moving.

As she rose from the floor, her face was shining with the glory of God; the love of God was beaming from her eyes and she was speaking in a language that was not Dutch – a heavenly language! The pastor, a Dutch Indonesian and a very short man, had been following me as I ministered. This giant of a woman, fixing her eyes on the pastor, marched toward him and enveloped him in her arms until he all but disappeared. As his face peered out from under her embrace, he gave me the definite look of, "Please! Rescue me!"

"It's new wine, Brother!" I called to him, and he began to laugh. (This was the first time I had seen the Dutch people laugh.) Leaving him, she went around hugging every man and woman in the room.

Nothing could have set the people free faster than when the Lord loosed this market gardener. Seeing the love of God in her face and the new wine of the Holy Spirit upon her, they knew she had received something wonderfully transforming, and they all wanted what she had.

What God did in that woman shook the whole area, and people came to her vegetable stand just to look at her – to see what great change God had wrought in her life. The word spread and I then had more invitations to preach than I could possibly fulfill.

Thus the new wine came to Holland, and Holland was receiving it. God did the very same thing for them as He did in England: they clapped their hands, danced in the Spirit, and got just as drunk in His presence as I had seen them do back home. I didn't think it was possible. As I stood before their long faces, the devil had said to me, "You've only got water as far as these people are concerned;" but I believed God had sent me. As I began to pour out, somewhere in the process, the water turned to wine and they were receiving it and being filled with great joy. God transforms with new wine!

Before I left, I saw the north of Holland change from mourning into a time of joy and dancing and freedom. Sickness and disease and devils were cast out in the name of Jesus. The rain was falling and there was a tremendous move of the Holy Spirit all around Hilversum, like they had never before seen or experienced. That mourning nation was visited by God, and upon all their suffering was poured new wine and fresh oil from the presence of the Lord!

When the Lord sent me to Holland, I was still broken-hearted and in mourning. The death of my mother had been a terrible blow, and I truly felt I could never smile again. For many, many months I found it difficult to preach joy while I was so bound; but during this low time the Lord broke into my life. He began to loose me in those farmhouse meetings in Devon, England, opening an entirely new dimension of ministry to me. As He poured out His Spirit upon the people, He also filled me and then sent me, full of the Holy Ghost, to Holland. With the blessing of God upon me and in the joy and strength of the Lord, all I had to do was start binding that spirit of depression that was upon the nation and loose them into the presence of God.

We may consider certain things in our lives to be negative, but there are no negatives, there are no accidents in God. And, we don't just "fall" into things. If there is a prayer born in our spirit, a hope, a dream, a promise that there is something for us in God, we must in yieldedness and obedience loose ourselves into His hand. God then takes the negatives — the things we do not understand or why they happened the way they did — and He purposefully and masterfully works out something far more wonderful than we could have imagined. Therefore, in God, sometimes it is first "no," then afterwards, it becomes a multiplied "yes," and we get much more than we ever asked for.

After Devon and Holland, I found that wherever I went, this blessing went with me: to Europe, across Canada and the States, and other places. Regardless of their language or the way the people looked or the color of their skin, it was the same new wine and the same presence of God filling them with joy and the love of God.

—ɱ—

In 1964, after driving 2400 miles from Florida to Oakland, California via Houston, I remember sitting in a pulpit in Oakland, thinking as I observed the people's faces, "I wonder what I have that they need?" I wasn't sure why the Lord had sent me. I was aware, however, that even if people appeared as if all was well, and even if the service was full of effervescence and shouting and dancing, that problems and unmet needs can still remain when the service is over. In the Oakland meetings, under the power of the Holy Spirit, it wasn't long before there came a melting of hearts and a pouring out of such a sweet anointing. Soon that anointing changed to new wine and, as the Spirit of God began to minister to the deeper needs of hearts and lives, the very same things began to happen there as had happened in other places.

One night the entire congregation of two or three hundred was slain in the Spirit. In the prayer time someone came up and put his hand on me, and I went down on the floor somewhere behind the pulpit. I don't remember another thing that happened that night because the Lord had taken over the meeting. At the end of the service an elderly black lady came to me and said, "You know, Sister Barbara, I was down on the floor, and when I got up there was nobody in their seats, just me! When I looked for you, I could see only your feet sticking out from behind the pulpit."

"What did you do then?" I asked her.

"I just got back down on the floor, 'cuz I didn't want to preach!"

"I feel like that, too – many times!" I told her.

Psalm 104:15 says that "wine makes glad the heart of man." This new wine represents the joy of the Holy Ghost, and from this joy comes our strength (Nehemiah 8:10). The precious anointing oil in Psalm 133 is likened to the softly distilling dew that fell upon Mount Hermon; and like oil upon the head that ran down Aaron's beard, covering him to the skirts of his garments. When there is an immersion into the wonderful anointing and joy of the Holy Ghost, the very depths of one's spirit and heart and life are touched and utterly transformed. One falls in love with Jesus – for that is what the anointing is: it is the love of God, His compassion, and also His power.

God ever calls us to higher realms in Him. The greater dimensions of His Spirit and of the heavenlies are made available to us through Jesus Christ. It is the work of the Holy Spirit to make these blessings a reality in our lives.

Jesus is our door to salvation and eternal life. God then gives us the gift of the Holy Spirit to lift us into new realms in Him. Many times I have been on an airliner that flies higher and higher above the clouds, until everything of earth becomes obscure. God wants us to rise into the spiritual and heavenly realm, where He dwells, and into a walk in the Spirit and a life in God above the natural and earthly.

The greatest way He has provided for us to come higher is through the ministry of His Spirit – not just a touch – but an ***immersion*** into the Holy Spirit that will bring us right up into the Shekinah Glory of God. I believe this is why the Lord sent the Holy Spirit and the new wine on the day of Pentecost: to lift the new church out of the natural and into the supernatural dimension of the Kingdom of God. His desire is not only to ***lift*** us into the heavenly realm, but to cause us to ***live*** there, also bringing others into that dimension.

Paul writes in I Corinthians 2:4 and 5,

> *"And my speech and my preaching was not with enticing words of man's wisdom, but in demonstration of the Spirit and of power: That your faith should not stand in the wisdom of men, but in the power of God."*

I believe that I should not only tell you of the goodness of God and all He is doing; but I should also tell you ***how*** to come in, and then ***bring*** you into what God is doing. If I preach on healing, I should demonstrate to you that God heals today and pray for you to be healed. If I preach on Holy Ghost fire, I should send you out of the meeting, burning. If I speak on fresh oil, I should send you out so anointed you can hardly keep your eyes open! If I preach on new wine, I should send you out drunk, not thirsty. That is the way the Holy Spirit works, for there is an impartation of the Word. God intends people to leave a meeting changed!

Over the years, since the Lord told me I would be a bearer of new wine and fresh oil, He has been faithful to pour out His Spirit wherever I have ministered. People from every land (some folk with much starch!) would fall from their chairs under the power of the Spirit. Lying on the floor unable to make their way back to their seats, they always looked just marvellous to me because of the joy of the Lord upon their faces. After such an overwhelming encounter in the river of God's glory, I knew their lives would be changed forever – and because of that I have never stopped smiling!

In Oakland, California 1964

Holland: Jewish Jeweler and wife, Anne, little man who opened the door of ministry in Holland, and Barbara

Barbara in Holland

In Holland: Barbara & Anne

Barbara preaching with her
Interpreter, Bella

Outside Bella's Home
In Holland

Chapter 12

Shortly before my trip to Holland in 1962, the Lord sent me back to Northern Ireland. My purpose in going, I thought, was to hold meetings; but the Lord had other plans. Soon after arriving, I did speak in a tiny country church just outside Belfast. In this meeting, unnoticed by me, was a woman sitting in the back of the church in a wheelchair. After preaching and praying for the folk who had come forward for prayer, I returned to Belfast.

Later that night, this woman was visited by an angel who said, "Send for… " The woman didn't hear a name, but instead heard a recording of my voice speaking. "Tell the preacher to come and she will speak God's Word to you," the angel said.

The next day, I was talking and praying in a Belfast hotel with the owners, a Brethren couple, about the baptism in the Holy Ghost. Later that evening, when I returned to the place where I was staying, the lady of the house met me at the door. In great excitement, she exclaimed, "They've sent for you! Five people arrived from the country today asking for you; they said an angel sent them. You have to go now!"

I said, "It's midnight! Country folk will be in bed by now. I'll go tomorrow." In the morning, feeling that I might be staying for a while, I packed all my belongings in the car and left for the country.

Driving out of Belfast to what seemed like the backwoods, I finally found the address that was given to me. Upon entering the house, I met a woman who had been afflicted with multiple sclerosis for twenty-one years. For the last five years she had been confined to a wheelchair. Now she was barely able to talk or to do anything for herself. I said to her, "I'm the one you sent for!"

Lodging was found for me in the attic of a lovely little farmhouse, just up the road from this woman. The attic was like Noah's ark: it had only one window—in the ceiling. You couldn't look out, just up! For a whole month, I retired to that little attic room to seek the Lord, free of all distractions; I could see neither person nor passing car, only sky!

At a certain time each day, I would go down and minister to this woman. At first, she could barely speak, and her sister would interpret for me what she was trying to say. Soon, marvellous things began to happen as the Holy Spirit began working miracles of healing and deliverance in her life from the multiple sclerosis.

After a few days, her jaw and face muscles began loosening, and I quickly came to the conclusion that the Lord was preparing her for the Baptism of the Holy Spirit. She was a Presbyterian and didn't know anything about the things of the Spirit, so I began to teach her out of Acts, chapter 2. "I believe God is opening your mouth," I told her. "Stay in Acts 2 and read it for yourself. Get ahold of what it says and expect something from God."

A short time later, when coming to the house one day, I found her bubbling over with excitement. Speaking very clearly now, she said to me, "I received what you were talking about. I've been praising the Lord and speaking in other tongues just like they did in Acts 2. It's wonderful! Jesus is wonderful!"

Then she said, "But, I don't know what I am going to do."

"What do you mean?" I asked.

"Well, the doctor visited and heard me praying in this new language, and every time I tried to speak with him, I couldn't speak in English! Not being a Christian, he was very upset and said to my sister, 'This is too much: multiple sclerosis and an insanity condition! We'll have to put her in an asylum.' Tomorrow he's bringing the minister with him as it takes two to sign the admission form. Now, what shall I do?"

Taking her hand, I said, "Let's pray." Then I agreed with her that these two men would not be able to move her into the asylum. Reassuring her I declared, "I don't know how the Lord will take care of you, but He will do something!"

The next day, anxious to know what had happened, I returned to her house and found her sitting in the wheelchair, smiling. "You're still here!" I said. "Yes!" she answered, "and the strangest thing happened. When the doctor and minister came I was wide awake, but just as they stepped through the door and I was about to say hello, sleep suddenly came over me. My eyelids became like lead and dropped down and I couldn't open my eyes. Then, I heard myself snoring loudly and couldn't stop. But I wasn't sleeping! I heard the minister say to the doctor, 'She looks peaceful to me.' And the doctor responded, 'Well, right now she's snoring, but you should see her when she is awake. Yesterday she was babbling and in an awful state.' 'Well,' said the minister, 'whatever the problem was yesterday it certainly is not present today. I don't think I can sign the form.'"

As the doctor and minister were talking, she continued snoring and kept trying to say, "I'm not sleeping!

I'm not sleeping!" However, the Lord had locked her mouth shut. As soon as they had gone and the door had closed behind them, her eyes popped open, and her sister said to her, "That was terrible of you, snoring like that in front of the doctor and minister."

"But I wasn't sleeping." she said.

"You weren't sleeping with your eyes shut and snoring like that? You were sound asleep!"

I said to the sister, "The Lord couldn't have done anything better. He put an anesthetic over her, shut her mouth and her eyes, then opened her nose and let her snore all the way through. While she was snoring away so peacefully, they didn't have the heart to put her into an asylum. What could they do with a snoring woman?"

Making a trip into Belfast one day, I missed my visit with this woman. The next day I arrived at the house at the usual time, knocked on the door and walked in. She greeted me with, "Is that you, Barbara?"

"Yes, it's me." I answered.

"Oh, I don't need you any more!"

"You don't need me any more? Well, that's good news," I replied, "because I must go to Holland soon."

She then asked "What perfume do you wear?"

"When I come to see you, I don't wear perfume! I just wash my face, comb my hair and come down the road," I replied.

"Then, I have something wonderful to tell you," she continued. "Yesterday, about 2:30, when you normally come, I was sitting and reading the Word. I heard the door open and close. I didn't look around, but just went on reading. Then I smelled your fragrance and I called out, 'How are you today, Barbara?' But no one was there."

"What fragrance?" I asked.

"Well," she said, "Every day when you arrive, a sweet fragrance arrives with you. I was sure it was your perfume. Yesterday, when I heard the door open, I couldn't see or hear anyone, but I smelt your fragrance. When I saw you weren't here, I realized the fragrance was not from you."

"What did it smell like?" I asked.

"Ah," she said, "I've never smelled anything like it… very sweet… very beautiful, like some Eastern perfume or spice…"

As she was trying to describe this spicy Eastern aroma, the Lord spoke Psalm 45:8 directly into my heart: "All Thy garments smell of myrrh, and aloes, and cassia." Suddenly, the Spirit quickened this verse to me. I realized then just how close I had been to those garments. Each day, as we were conversing about the things of the Spirit, the Lord had drawn near. I never smelled Him myself, but the Lord had opened her spirit to sense the smell of His garments. When I didn't come that day and she was alone reading His Word, the Lord kept the date, manifesting His presence to her as a sweet fragrance.

I said to her, "When the Lord walks in and reveals Himself to you, you surely don't need me!"

I learned something of the presence of God in a remarkable way through my experience with this woman, and I locked that secret in my heart. A few years later, in 1964, when the Lord gave me an eight-week revival in a church in Houston, Texas, God began to manifest this phenomenon in a much greater way. Each night the revival meeting would last until quite late, but after the meeting was dismissed, there would always be those who would linger at the altar under the presence of God.

One night, after most folk had gone, I noticed some who were praying around the altar were beginning to sniff, as if they were smelling something. I then watched as some on one side of the platform wrinkled their noses and sniffed, and in another area others were doing the same. Once again, the Lord spoke to me, "All Thy garments smell of myrrh, and aloes, and cassia." Remembering the woman in Ireland, I asked the people if they smelled something. They replied that a very sweet, delicate fragrance seemed to waft by, coming and going as if in waves.

Relating the story of the Irish woman, I explained that if we wanted the Lord to linger, it was important to stay in an atmosphere of worship. Then, as we continued to worship, the Lord continued to walk among us as through His garden, leaving the sweet scent of His garments as He passed by. Though we were there until the early hours of the morning, it seemed like only moments in His wonderful Presence.

As the Houston meetings progressed over the next weeks, many others smelled the heavenly fragrance. Some who didn't, but saw what was happening, came up to the altar to sniff. The presence of God, however, cannot be smelled through the natural senses alone. Rather, it is a spiritual revelation, manifested to our natural senses.

I was thankful that the Lord had given me the experience in Ireland to help me understand this manifestation of His presence. Although I had never smelled it myself, I could help them to know what to do when His presence came in that way — it was time to worship Him! Had we talked or simply ignored Him, His presence would have lifted and we would have missed those precious, unforgettable, eternal moments with Him.

Many times we can be near something wonderful in the Holy Spirit but, through lack of understanding, we can grieve Him. And when the Spirit of God lifts, we have no covering; there is nothing we can do, for all the movings of God are supernatural. He pours out His Spirit in His own way; and we must be ready and knowledgeable in the ways of His Spirit, otherwise we will miss Him.

Our spirit man must be in tune with His Spirit. When God is moving, or about to do something, if we withdraw from people, pray and even fast a meal, our spirit will become more sensitive to His Spirit. We can then come to church "in tune" and not to "get tuned." When we come tuned up and prayed up, we will be ready for a visitation from God! As the Holy Spirit moves in our meetings, and we keep our worship flowing unto Him, yielding our spirits to His in an attitude of humility and dependence, He will flow through us revealing Himself and His Glory."

In Exodus 30:22-25, God instructed Moses to create a beautiful anointing oil by combining specific measurements of olive oil, myrrh, cassia and other ingredients. Especially prepared with holy hands in the house of the apothecary, this lovely ointment produced a beautiful fragrance, and was called *the Holy Anointing Oil.* It was used only to anoint the vessels of the tabernacle and to anoint priests and kings.

Psalm 45:7,8 "Thou lovest righteousness, and hatest wickedness: therefore, God, thy God hath anointed thee with the oil of gladness above thy fellows. All thy garments smell of myrrh, and aloes, and cassia, out of the ivory palaces, whereby they have made thee glad."

This scripture is speaking of our Lord Jesus Christ and of the garments that surround Him. As our heavenly High Priest, His garments are holy and heavily anointed, and the very fragrance of that anointing is upon Him.

As that precious ointment was poured upon the head of Aaron the high priest, and ran down his beard to the skirts of his garments, so the anointing upon our heavenly High Priest flows down upon us, His "fellows," and our spiritual garments are then anointed with that same Spirit. With this anointing upon us, we also have the opportunity and privilege of radiating this heavenly fragrance.

It is a marvellous thing when we can go to a place and, under this precious anointing, leave a fragrance behind – a fragrance neither found in a bottle nor made by man, but something from the apothecaries of Glory. This fragrance is one of the treasures of this garment, and is the inward, fine detailed work of His Spirit. It is so subtle that you don't know exactly when or how it happens.

We need not be afraid to ask for the supernatural in our ministry. Mark 16:17 says "these signs shall follow them that believe." We don't have to work signs – they follow those who believe. If we will just be our natural selves and walk with God, He will put the supernatural in our ministries that will affect something life-changing and eternal for His people.

When the Lord first imparted His gifts to me, the words, "I believe God," were burned into my heart by the Holy Spirit. As I stepped out in the beginnings of my ministry and was met with misunderstanding, opposition, persecution, and personal heartbreak, I kept walking with God and believing Him for the impossible. It is wonderful now to turn around and see following in my train, miracle after miracle: God working with me. Can you think of anything more gracious, anything more beautiful, anything more fulfilling than *God working with you!*

In 1965, Barbara and Anne first stopped by Elim Bible Institute for an early morning prayer meeting. After the meeting, Barbara gave a prophetic word to Wade Taylor, a man whom she had never met, that one day he would have a Bible school and it would be located in upstate New York.

In His Divine plan, God arranged for Pinecrest Bible Training Center in Salisbury Center, New York, founded by Wade Taylor in 1968, to become Barbara's home and ministry base in the United States through the 1970's and 80's, until she returned to Stafford, England in 1993.

It was in this Bible school that Barbara's anointing and ministry was sown into the hearts of another generation. Her prophetic word and ministry of new wine and fresh oil opened a dimension of the Spirit that carried hearts to higher vistas, revealing greater possibilities than hitherto imagined; for "eye hath not seen… but God reveals by His Spirit."

The deep of God's heart forever calls out. Barbara Massie's ministry inspired lives to respond; to reach for that vision and calling of knowing and walking with God, led by His Spirit; and to touch that dimension in the heart of God where His River runs full and free with the purity of the heavenly. Through Barbara Massie's ministry, another generation was enabled by His Spirit to apprehend the unfolding will and purpose of God for their day.

And the River flows on...

Part Three

Testimonies

With David Greenow

Evangelist David Greenow

I entered Bible college in Penygroes, South Wales in January 1950, and found that one of the students was a certain Miss Barbara Massie. It was of interest to me because on May 25, 1942, I had a very personal encounter with the Lord Jesus in which I passed from spiritual death unto life. The minister in that service was Pastor W. W. Massie, who was Barbara's father. He won several of us young people to the Lord that Pentecost weekend. Through the Bible college contact, I was privileged to get to know the other members of the Massie family, and it was a joy later to share ministry with Barbara and her sister Anne. They were widely known as the "Massie sisters" and blessed many with their ministry in song. It became clearer, with the passage of time, that Barbara not only was developing a good ministry in the Word, but also a prophetic ministry with considerable clarity and edge. When I mention her name to people today, they often say that they received a prophetic word through her that was later wonderfully fulfilled, sometimes years later!

I am sure that what helped bring Barbara's ministry forth, and gave her courage as a woman to take her place in speaking forth God's Word, was what happened in May of 1951. There were two pastors from Wales who had spent some years ministering in the States and Canada, and had been greatly affected by what was then called "the latter rain anointing." These brothers visited the Bible college to share their hearts with us – students and staff; and we experienced the Holy Spirit in latter rain visitation in a way never to be forgotten. After they had ministered God's Word, we felt a tremendous brokenness and a deep repentance toward God and each other. We came forth from that time with an awareness of the current moving of the Holy Spirit in revival on the earth. Sister Barbara, and any of us who experienced this, were never the same again. There was an urge to seek the face of God, from which a spontaneous chain of prayer and fasting resulted, and continued until the end of college and beyond.

Some controversy arose because of the blessing within the church circles we moved in; but Sister Barbara seemed to find new strength and boldness during that time. She and I, along with others, ministered together in missions and special services, which often knew rich times of anointing and Divine visitation.

A team of us took over an old unused cinema, in February and March of 1960, for six weeks of evangelistic outreach. We were told there had been no mission of any kind in that area for over thirty years. There were very few in attendance that first week, but Sister Barbara prophesied that there would be an increase. The next week and the weeks that followed, we had an influx of both young and older people. Several came to the Lord, and Barbara's ministry and practical help was much appreciated at the time.

I moved to the north of Ireland in March of 1952 and then in 1954 a mighty visitation of God's power came to that country. In '55 I was invited to take a mission for two weeks in a certain place and was there for twenty months. Sister Barbara joined us and brought a ministry that had both clarity and relevance. She visited other places in both Ireland and Britain, and those who remember her still speak of her ministry with deep appreciation. She often spoke of her desire to visit and minister in the States. We often joked about what would happen when she "hit the States!" She did go to the United States and affected many lives with her anointed ministry, thus many on both sides of the Atlantic and beyond are grateful for her life and ministry.

Barbara often spoke and sang about the river of God, and truly her life and ministry were profoundly touched by His river.

Evangelist David Greenow,
Conference Speaker,
Portadown, Co. Armagh, Northern Ireland

Pastor Gordon McGee

Our church, Houston Gospel Tabernacle, here in the city of Houston, Texas, experienced a most gracious and powerful visitation of God during the visit of Sister Barbara Massie. Undoubtedly God came down among us during those eight weeks of our sister's visit with us.

Sister Barbara was a called and consecrated woman of God with a great anointing of the Spirit of the Lord upon her life and her ministry. She was an evangelist and certainly a prophetess of the Lord and left behind a rich spiritual legacy after her time with us!

God sent her to our church — and I can make this statement without any reservation of any sort. We didn't write to her and invite her, and most certainly she did not invite herself! God simply brought her our way two weeks prior to Christmas 1963. It was by a remarkable set of circumstances that the Lord brought us together in His will, and I bless God for the day Sister Massie crossed the threshold of our church!

Her visit signaled an extraordinary outpouring of blessing and a visitation of God. Repeatedly, before her coming, the Lord had warned us to prepare our hearts for His visitation. When it came, we were extremely blessed and thrilled at His moving.

There were many outstanding features to that revival, with diverse miraculous workings of God and physical healings of various sicknesses and diseases. There were many with back problems, diabetes, blindness, and even cancers that the Lord touched and healed at that time.

I recall that, initially, the Lord directed us in glorious Jericho marches as the people marched around and around the church giving glory to God; some shouted and some were weeping while others sang God's praises as they marched. Those were glorious scenes!

This was followed by another phase of the revival which our people called "the weight of glory." I certainly accepted Sister Barbara's explanation of it being fresh oil from heaven that the Lord was pouring upon His people.

I remember some visitors were skeptical about falling out under the power of the Spirit. They thought that it was simply emotionalism. It was, however, interesting to see folks who came forward for prayer and were determined to resist falling. It seems to me they were the ones who instantly fell as hands were laid upon them in the Name of the Lord!

One wonderful feature of that visitation of God was that it attracted ministers from such a wide radius. I knew of over forty pastors who were drawn in from various denominations and from scattered points who were ministered to and then returned to their churches with the fire of the Lord upon their lives. As I think back, that revival was never advertised or heralded in advance in any way, yet God drew in many people and ministers like a magnet! During that time the Lord raised up several of our young men and filled their hearts to go out and preach. Today they are evangelists out in the harvest!

One unique experience in a meeting I shall never forget, for it was so unusual. Most of the people had left the service because the hour was so late. People were down at the altar praying and some began to smell the garment of the Lord as He walked among them. Did not the sacred writer say, "All of His garments smell of myrrh and aloe and cassia?" The first one to notice the fragrance was a young Irish woman who had been slain under the power of God. As she lay on the carpet, she became aware of this beautiful aroma. After she arose, she shared with a few at the altar only to find that others, too, were noticing it. I had knelt down at the altar myself some distance off from the others to pray. I also caught a waft of the most delicate fragrance and then it seemed to pass. After another minute or two, the aroma again came and went as if "someone" were passing by. It was the personal presence of the Lord Jesus! I have never forgotten this blessing from the Lord, as it was a sacred occasion. Some had the impulse to remove their shoes as it seemed the ground on which we stood was indeed holy!

A spirit of revelation came during those days and many were given beautiful songs and choruses under the inspiration of the Holy Spirit! Those songs remained as a rich spiritual legacy and reminder of our sister's time with us. Our church was never the same after this visitation of the Spirit of God.

Rev. Gordon McGee,
Former Pastor,
Houston Gospel Tabernacle, Houston, Texas

Charles & Maureen Price

It was a privilege to have known Evangelist Barbara Massie for almost 30 years. I first came in contact with her through the late Norman Evans. We received a real refreshing in the Holy Spirit as Sister Massie ministered for us when I was pastoring in London before going to Scotland. One of the lovely songs she sang for us at Faith Temple in London was that dear old hymn "Gathering Flowers for the Master's Bouquet," along with "I Am Going to a City Where the Roses Never Fade." She is blest to have made it to the shores of Glory ahead of us! What an inspiration she was to all of us that came in contact with her, and she is greatly missed!

It was precious how the Lord raised her up among the early Apostolics in the days when women weren't too well accepted. She was a pioneer in the end-time and latter rain message that has now circled the globe.

Barbara and Anne would stay with us in our home in London several times during the early days of her ministry. We were privileged to take her and receive her from the airport on many of her mission trips abroad.

I recall one of the places she spoke of when God directed her to the Houston, Texas area. She held a crusade there at the Elim church for the late Rev. Gordon McGee (formerly from Northern Ireland.) She first went there for a few nightly meetings, but ended up staying for over six weeks, as she was used mightily in healings, miracles & gifts of prophecy.

Rev. Charles T. & Maureen Price,
North Wales

With Kenneth Logie

Pastor Kenneth Logie

I appreciated working with Sister Barbara Massie during those weeks of God's visitation in 1964. Sometime before her arrival I was speaking with another minister here in California concerning having guest ministers in our churches. He said to me, "Brother Logie, it is so hard to find an evangelist that you can trust." After Barbara Massie left, Sister Logie wrote a letter to this pastor and said, "Now we have had an evangelist here at Gospel Chapel that we can trust! I believe this evangelist works according to the will of God and righteously." This is one reason why I am so glad that I had the privilege of working with Sister Barbara.

I recall one morning, in particular, as we sat on the platform during the service, the offering was being taken. Sister Barbara turned to me and said, "Brother Logie, here are some tithes that someone gave to me before the meeting began." She then passed it to me. I replied, "Well, thank you!" I thanked her because I believe that there is a right way and a wrong way the Lord's ministers can operate. That single act has given me more confidence in our sister than all the messages I have heard here at the Chapel. Our sister moved in the upright way of doing things. We continued to pray God's blessing upon Barbara's life, long after she left. Our desire was that she would always be truly blessed of the Lord and that the doors of Gospel Chapel in Oakland would always be open to her, though the Lord never directed her to return to us on this side of glory!

Rev. Kenneth Logie,
Oakland, CA

Pastor Bernard and Sharon Evans

It was an early spring evening, during the late sixties, when we first met Sister Barbara Massie. We had been working with Clair Hutchins, founder of the now well-known Brooklyn Tabernacle and it's sister church in Newark, New Jersey. Our assignment had been to oversee the Newark congregation, and brother Hutchins had recommended Sister Massie for special meetings. Little did we realize that this woman of God would become a provision of the Lord to our ministry, not just then but also in years to come.

In those early days, we were to discover that her delivery in the pulpit carried a freshness that drew hearts to a gracious Saviour. She loved the sense of flowing in the "new wine" and we were drawn to love Him the more. As the series of meetings came to a close, the Lord gave her a prophetic vision of violence coming to the city, of flames, rioting and civil unrest. The Lord prepared us so that in the heat of that summer, as the city was exploding into a war zone, we were able to walk without fear.

Much later, in another congregation we were pastoring, Sister Barbara prophesied concerning the coming revival in Eastern Europe. A large number of refugees attending the service, who'd only recently fled that area, sat in stunned silence as a translator repeated the words for their benefit. They were all too familiar with the godless grip of Communism's tyranny — yet, it has come to pass. Revival is indeed sweeping through eastern European nations.

Her prophetic ministry to us, concerning our own future, spoke clearly that we would be serving even as we are in this present position. Though at the time it seemed so unlikely that this would ever come to pass, events proved otherwise twenty years later.

This, of course, is only a brief peek at the significant ministry and mentoring that characterized her life. Her respect for the anointing of the Holy Spirit was resolute. Out of this poise of heart, the Lord continued to pour Himself through her, even in seasons when she might've wished for time out.

One more personal note, the Lord seemed to knit Sister Barbara (and her lovely sister, Anne) into the fabric of our family. What had begun as providing a place to stay in our home when she came to minister, turned into a home-away-from-home for her on other occasions. We discovered that she was a gifted story-teller and comedienne. She would regale us with tales of her childhood, of nursing school days, and of her experiences as a midwife in Scotland. She'd spin out these stories in her lilting brogue until we'd be aching from laughter and begging for more.

Such a gifted individual would have to have idiosyncrasies and perhaps foibles that would not go unnoticed, but as we came to know her even more intimately, our respect and affection for her only increased. She was solid in the Word and in relationship with her Lord. We're grateful for the years of fellowship that we've been able to enjoy; our lives have truly been enriched.

Rev. Bernard and Sharon Evans,
President of Elim Fellowship, Lima, NY

Pastor Joseph Nettleton

I had many opportunities to be with Barbara during the years she was in New York State. I have many great memories of her ministry. The two I remember the most were in1967 and 1975.

While I was a student at Elim Bible Institute in 1967, Barbara was a guest speaker and taught on the New Wine. God poured out the new wine one night upon the student body. Many in attendance got drunk on the new wine from heaven. People were lying all over the platform and the steps to the platform. Many were laughing and staggering like drunken sailors. It was a joyous occasion. Since the Toronto Blessing has now impacted many around the world, much more is now understood about this type of outpouring. Back in 1967 it was very radical. No one we knew was flowing in this type of anointing other than Barbara Massie. Barbara was a forerunner by twenty-five years in the outpouring of the Holy Spirit.

In 1975, while pastoring in Depauville, NY, Barbara was invited to speak in our church on a Sunday morning. That Sunday a young couple providentially attended the church for the first time, knowing only one other person in the congregation. When Barbara ministered she called this couple up to the front of the church. While they were walking up, she (by a word of knowledge) told them they were going to receive money in the mail. The couple got excited and said, "It already came in the mail!" Barbara said, "No, you will get more this week."

She then noticed the two year old child the mother was holding was severely disabled. Barbara took the child and prayed for a complete healing. She also prophesied that they would be used greatly by the Lord, and then sent them back to their seats.

That afternoon we received a call from the couple, and they said their two year old sat up for the first time in his life. The next day they called and said the baby sat up for two hours, and by the end of the week he sat up all day. He soon began walking. A month later they took the baby to the specialist in Rochester, New York. The doctor looked at the baby's chart and explained to the parents the problems the child had at birth, the problems the child had at six months, at one year and at eighteen months. During his checking the two year old, he kept saying, "Amazing!" Several times during the examination he said, "Amazing." At the end of the session he wrote across the charts "Remarkable Recovery… removed from my care!"

The first week after Barbara spoke, the couple came to me and said they had received money in the mail every day that week. I was the only person in the church who knew them, and I did not send them any money!

This couple became members of the church and also developed a significant ministry. The husband wrote a dramatic play for Easter about the crucifixion as seen through the eyes of the Centurion Soldier. Over the years, hundreds if not thousands of people have been saved while watching this play. As Barbara Massie was very influential in the working of God in this couple's lives, so she also has an inheritance in the lives of all those who have been touched by their ministry.

Rev. Joseph E. Nettleton,
Director, US Ministries Dept.,
Elim Fellowship, Lima, New York

June 2001 Anne with Allan and Marie Littzi
Pastors of Hope of Prayer Christian Ministries
Nanticoke, PA

Pastor Marie Littzi

Proof, if proof were ever needed, of God's encompassing generational love and compassion, can be clearly seen in Barbara's ordained meeting with Marie Littzi at Kingston, Pennsylvania in 1974. What has flowed from that first encounter, by touching so many lives, can only be described as truly miraculous and truly of God. It also reveals the ongoing, transferable power of the Lord's anointing to those vessels who are open to receive.

Marie came along to Barbara's meeting that night knowing no one, but knowing she had a need only God could reach. She went forward in faith after hearing Barbara preach even though she was not prepared for what was going on around her. As she made her way through people lying prostrate across the floor under the tangible power of God, she pressed in, believing this was her chance to have a new and deeper encounter with the living God.

She told Barbara of her prognosis, which was not good in the eyes of man, and the uncertain future this presented. Diagnosed with kidney disease, she faced the prospect of surgery with ongoing medication for the rest of her life and an end to any further childbearing. Barbara brought her before the Lord and prayed healing for her body and release for her spirit. She also advised Marie to go back to the doctors and have her healing confirmed. Marie went home that night to her husband Allan and their children, Allan and Carolann, knowing she had been touched and healed. It took the following year to convince the skeptical clinicians, and even though they were amazed by her health and vibrancy, surgery was still to be their option. Only when the urologist had fresh X-rays taken, and compared them to what had showed up before, was her total healing confirmed. He could not explain what had happened but was delighted to give her a clean bill of health. Marie and Allan celebrated by going on to complete their family with two more healthy sons, John and Aaron.

Marie and Barbara kept in touch becoming close and lifelong friends. This caused Allan a few problems, when the lady evangelist came to visit. Pretty much your stereo-typical male, Allan enjoyed a beer, a smoke, and his TV sports, preferably uninterrupted. So too much of this 'God talk' in his own home had him feeling the pressure, as Barbara's visits became more frequent. When Barbara spoke to him about the Lord, he would be in full retreat saying, "I don't want to hear this."

But the Lord had plans for Allan and Marie and gave Barbara a prophetic word for him which would have seemed impossible in the natural. "The Lord shall bring you down to ashes. Through this you shall come up as an eagle. You will have compassion for others. You will not be a millionaire in the natural, but you will be a millionaire in the spiritual. The devil would have killed you were it not for the hand of the Lord. Yours will be a prophetic ministry. You have not to struggle; the Lord is doing the work. Put away all the things that are not of the Lord. Do not touch the unclean things and the Lord will restore health to your body."

Allan's response on hearing this was to say, "Tell her to be quiet. I don't want to hear her saying these things." Barbara would respond by saying,"...but you're our pastor," or "Preacher, come here," which brought further pleas of, "Don't be prophesying over me any more." But God's word was sure and as Al answered

God's call on his life, he was healed of chronic stomach pains that had plagued his life.

The fulfillment of Barbara's words was complete when her sister, Anne, visited America in June 2001. Staying with Marie's mom, Caroline, she was taken to the House of Prayer Fellowship in Nanticoke, PA, for a "Night of Remembrance" service in honor of Barbara. Outside the church she was greeted by Allan, and her response was, "What are you doing here?" To which he replied, "I am the pastor!" Stunned, Anne exclaimed the words by which we all seek to limit God, "I don't believe it!" Having met the old Allan, she perhaps had cause to be taken by surprise. On reflection Anne was later to think, "O ye of little faith."

At this remembrance service, people were lining up to testify how the power God used to touch their lives through Barbara, was still at work in them, and still effective as they ministered to others. Story after story unfolded how lives and situations were changed through the ministry of this woman from Scotland. She had come to America in obedience and through necessity, as the church in the United Kingdom was not ready in those days for women in ministry.

Barbara had something inside her that could not, nor was meant to be contained. It can all be seen as part of God's incredible plan to reach into many lives through one willing and obedient servant. Marie's mom and late father came to saving faith, as did her and Allan's four grown children, along with countless others whom we may never know until we ourselves get to glory. When the Lord asks, "Whom shall we send?" Our reply should be as Barbara's was, "Here am I Lord, send me!"

Rev. Marie Littzi,
Kingston, PA

Wade E. Taylor

As a student in Bible school, I was privileged to participate in a major visitation of the Lord. During the latter part of this visitation, a fountain of new wine appeared in the Spirit. I partook of this new wine in abundance and my life was changed. As I had always been bound within myself and withdrawn, I found the new wine liberated me, and set me free to obey the Lord, even in difficult situations. Thus, I placed substantial value on this experience.

In January 1967, while teaching at Elim Bible Institute, a visitor named Barbara Massie came to the school one Sunday. I was in charge of the chapel service, and invited her to speak. She ministered on the new wine. Some didn't understand her ministry, but I did; and I made room for her to continue ministering in the Sunday services. The Lord moved mightily through her in impartation of new wine, and lives were transformed and ministries birthed.

In 1970, after Pinecrest Bible Training Center was formed, Barbara Massie came to the school; and again the Lord mightily used her in the pouring out of the new wine. Lives to this day testify of the impartation of the Spirit and the transformation that took place in them through her ministry.

Dr. Wade E. Taylor,
Founder of Pinecrest
Bible Training Center,
Salisbury Center, New York

Pastor Julie Grove

Pages could easily be filled expressing the influence of Barbara Massie's ministry in my life. To this day I can hear her prophetic voice resounding in my heart, a voice of spiritual authority, a creative voice, speaking into being the foundation of the ministry God purposed for me. The impartation of anointing I received during every service she ministered at Pinecrest Bible Training Center has continued to bring increase for over 33 years.

Sister Massie's weighty anointing and intense prophetic word, I believe, birthed the expression of the Spirit of God in my ministry. I am eternally grateful for her life, and thankful for her willingness to pay the price to wear with grace her powerful prophetic mantle.

May God raise up in this generation lives also willing to pay the price for such depth of anointing and authority in the Spirit.

Julie A. Grove,
Pastor of Integrity
Christian Fellowship
Taylor, Michigan

At Pinecrest
Bible Training Center
with Alan Deppe

Alan Deppe
Class of 1975, Pinecrest Bible Training Center

There is a River, the streams whereof shall make glad the city of God.

Psalm 46:4

Barbara Massie was one that was in "God's River," always encouraging the streams to flow. Glad was the heart of God when they did. Yes, the pride of intellect had to go, and that was hard for me to accept. It didn't quite make sense, yet it was God and He doesn't always make sense. Her life was a precious testimony and her prophetic words were powerful.

So finally the day came when the stream burst forth. I have never been the same! The well that has been set free has brought clear, clean, healing waters beyond anything man can do. A new sense and experience of the anointing changed my life. "There is a River" and Barbara Massie was one that the Lord used to cause the streams to flow in my life. And for that I will always be grateful!

Alan Deppe,
Wooster, Ohio

Birthday Party with Pinecrest students standing: Teacher Joseph Nieves

Pastor John Scaduto

In the Spring of 1974, four newly saved rock and roll musicians strolled into Pinecrest Retreat Center in Setauket, New York. Little did these former drug addicts realize how radically affected their lives would become by their first encounter with a Scottish woman by the name of Sister Barbara Massie.

To this day it remains a mystery to me how this woman of God could see beyond our outward appearance and perceive any real destiny of God for our lives. Let's face it, we obviously were not dressed and groomed appropriately for a religious service. We were hippies, you know – long hair, beards, sneakers and jeans, our very best Sunday going to meeting clothes!

And while most people were checking to make sure their pocketbooks and children were kept safe from us, Barbara was drawing nearer to us and getting in tune with God's voice. (We found out later that God had already prepared Barbara for this first encounter and told her she would meet people in America that would be used of God in their generation.)

You could always tell when Barbara was in the Spirit, by that other-worldly look in her eyes. Her prophetic utterance over our lives seemed a bit much at times, and in some ways even embarrassing. She must be mistaken! Doesn't she see the sin and failure that everyone else sees? How can she make these predictions over our lives? How could a Holy God ever use us? How?

We later learned that Barbara looked at people through the eyes of Jesus. She looked beyond our faults and saw our destinies. Barbara was unusually comfortable with these four societal non-conformists. We didn't understand the protocols of church behavior, and she was fine with that and found it quite harmless and very amusing.

Speaking of amusing, long before Rodney Howard Brown ever came on the scene, Barbara and her precious sister, Anne, were ministering the new wine to a new generation. New wine poured into new wine skins. As with most prophets, Barbara was a woman ahead of her time and was a pioneer to this present day prophetic movement. It cost her dearly to live the life of a prophetic sojourner, but she never complained; she was a soldier in the Lord's army. Her words over our lives came to pass, and today four lowly sinners have become four grateful servants of Christ. We will never forget the touch from the mantle of Sister Barbara Massie.

Rev. Robert Taoromina, Pastor
of New Covenant Church;
Rev. Barry Taylor, Minister of Music at
Massapequa Tabernacle;
Rev. Anthony D'Onofrio, Bishop and Founding Pastor of
Upper Room Christian World Center;
Rev. John Scaduto, Pastor/Prophet at
Upper Room Christian World Center'
Dix Hills, NY

Pastor Robert Taoromina

I met Sister Barbara Massie at Pinecrest Setauket in March of 1974, the month I received Christ. It was there that I received my first prophecy from her. Over the next two years, while I attended Pinecrest Bible Training Center in Salisbury Center, New York, that word proved to have a profound influence in guiding my steps.

Her guidance in the first years of my preparing for ministry helped me keep the focus on my calling to win the lost and disciple them. She always ministered with great compassion to the troubled soul. And, of course, every meeting was filled with the "new wine" of the Holy Spirit.

I'll always remember the joy of the Lord in every meeting. Her devotion as a handmaiden of the Lord is an inspiration to us all.

Barbara was a forerunner of the modern renewal movement that places such emphasis on the joy of the Lord. Many of the same manifestations of the Holy Spirit that have characterized the Toronto and Pensacola meetings of the mid-nineties were evident in her meetings at Pinecrest in the early seventies.

Who would have ever guessed that the laughter, new wine, joy, and prophetic flow in her meetings would end up spilling over to the mainstream of the move of God in the next generation! Certainly not some of her peers who misunderstood her calling as a winebibber for the Lord! I guess we have all learned to drink deeply of the Spirit of God (and laugh a lot) from Sister Barbara.

I remember her preaching and warning all to, "...touch not the Oil or the Wine." She was right. Nothing and no one can stop the outpouring of the Oil and New Wine in these latter days! I'm sure she is laughing now!

Rev. Robert Taoromina, Pastor,
New Covenant Church, East Meadow, N.Y.

Pastor Anthony D'Onofrio

When I first met Sister Barbara, I had just been delivered and set free from the rock and drug culture. My clothes fit the bill and you couldn't possibly fit my hairdo into a potato sack! In those days I was reeking of marijuana, and the stain of the world was still visible upon me. Yet, through her prophetic eye, she perceived in me what I could not perceive in myself — a call to the ministry, prophesying the office of a pastor, the building, the people, even the locality! The Lord through His vessel, impregnated a vision in my heart, which I am now seeing unfold before my eyes.

Rev. Anthony D'Onofrio,
Bishop and Founding Pastor of
Upper Room Christian World Center,
Dix Hills, N.Y.

1974 with John Scaduto, Robert Taoromina, Barry Taylor, and Anthony D'Onofrio

1984 with Robert Taoromina, John Scaduto and Anthony D'Onofrio

At Pinecrest with Wade and Mae Taylor

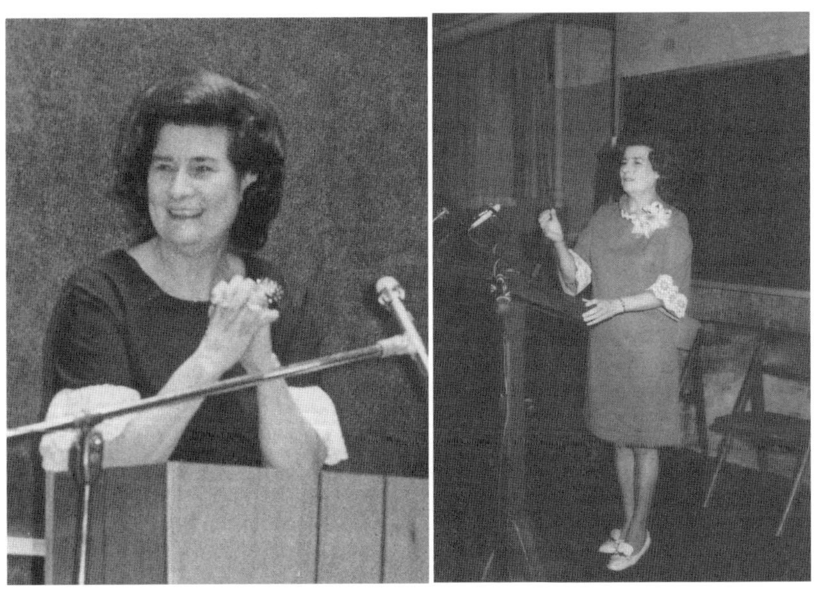

Ministry at Pinecrest Bible Training Center

1984 Banquet in Barbara's Honor, Long Island, New York
Bernard Evans, Wade Taylor, Anne, Barbara, John Scaduto, Anthony D'Onofrio

Wade Taylor, Anne, Barbara, Craig Rustey, Anthony D'Onofrio

With Stan Smith, Chris Burlingame Vizzo, Tom Worth, Anne, Peggy Boyle, Phil Gauthier, Barbara O'Conner Caisse, Marsha Worth

Wade Taylor, Barbara and Bernard Evans

Stanley Smith, Ray DeliCarpini, Barbara, Rudy Migliori and Anthony D'Onofrio

Barbara and Anne